Contemporary Cost Management

MASAYASU TANAKA
Science University of Tokyo, Japan

TAKEO YOSHIKAWA
Yokohama National University, Japan

JOHN INNES
University of Dundee, UK

FALCONER MITCHELL
University of Edinburgh, UK

CHAPMAN & HALL
University and Professional Division

London · Glasgow · Weinheim · New York · Tokyo · Melbourne · Madras

Published by Chapman & Hall, 2–6 Boundary Row, London SE1 8HN

Chapman & Hall, 2–6 Boundary Row, London SE1 8HN, UK

Blackie Academic & Professional, Wester Cleddens Road, Bishopbriggs, Glasgow G64 2NZ, UK

Chapman & Hall GmbH, Pappelallee 3, 69469 Weinheim, Germany

Chapman & Hall USA, One Penn Plaza, 41st Floor, New York NY 10119, USA

Chapman & Hall Japan, Thomson Publishing Japan, Hirakawacho Nemoto Building, 6F, 1–7–11 Hirakawa-cho, Chiyoda-ku, Tokyo 102, Japan

Chapman & Hall Australia, Thomas Nelson Australia, 102 Dodds Street, South Melbourne, Victoria 3205, Australia

Chapman & Hall India, R. Seshadri, 32 Second Main Road, CIT East, Madras 600 035, India

First edition 1993
First published in paperback 1994

© 1993 M. Tanaka, T. Yoshikawa, J. Innes and F. Mitchell

Typeset in 11/13 Palatino by Pure Tech Corporation, Pondicherry, India
Printed in Great Britain by TJ Press Ltd, Padstow, Cornwall

ISBN 0 412 60320 9

A catalogue record for this book is available from the British Library

Library of Congress Cataloging-in-Publication data available
Contemporary cost management / Masayasu Tanaka . . .[et al.].—1st ed.
　　　p. cm.
　　Includes bibliographical references and index
　　ISBN 0–412–45210–3
　　1. Cost control.　2.Cost accounting.　I. Tanaka, Masayasu.
　HD47.3.C64　　1992
　658.15'52—dc20　　　　　　　　　　　　　　　　92–30646
　　　　　　　　　　　　　　　　　　　　　　　　　　　CIP

∞ Printed on permanent acid-free text paper, manufactured in accordance with the proposed ANSI/NISO Z 39.48–199X and ANSI Z 39.48-1984

Contents

Preface

We have all been involved in research and teaching in the area of costing and cost management over the last two decades. During this time the discipline of management accounting at both the academic and practical levels has become increasingly dynamic, largely in response to managerial developments such as total quality management, just-in-time and computer integrated manufacture. A range of new techniques has emerged and management accountants have proved increasingly adept at adapting traditional techniques to fit modern circumstances. This text draws on the experiences of East and West to outline how these developments contribute to contemporary cost management. This new paperback edition has also provided us with an opportunity to make some modifications to the original text, particularly in respect of updating source reference material.

CHAPTER ONE

Introduction

This book brings together some of the ideas and practices which are currently employed in Japan and in the West to improve cost-effectiveness and so enhance competitiveness. In order to provide a foundation for this, Chapter 2 outlines the conventional views taken by accountants of cost and cost management and Chapter 3 provides a review of the nature of traditional costing which will be of use particularly to non-accountant readers wishing to appreciate how the contemporary approaches supplement what already exists.

The Japanese emphasis on cost management has focused on the pre-production stages in a product's life cycle when the key decisions on product design, resourcing and production technology are all being made, and when up to 90% of a product's total costs are committed. The use of target costing (Chapter 4), functional analysis (Chapter 5), cost estimation (Chapter 6) and cost tables (Chapter 7) all evidence their determination to 'get cost right' before production commences. In the West more effort has been placed on the assessment of actual costs incurred after production is underway. Activity-based costing has received great attention since the mid-1980s as the most recent approach to this type of analysis. It provides a methodology for costing product lines (Chapter 8) and for directing managerial attention to areas where action may result in cost benefit to the organization concerned (Chapter 9).

Finally, both in Japan and in the West the need to manage stocks and to produce output in a fast, reliable and flexible manner have been increasingly recognized as an essential component of maintaining a competitive position (Chapter 10). The need to integrate market and situational information in the internal cost-based analyses presented to management has also been globally promoted as providing an important input at the strategic level (Chapter 11).

Thus, this book covers the main aspects of management accountants' potential contribution towards the support and maintenance of their organization as a world class provider of goods or services.

CHAPTER TWO

Cost and cost management

INTRODUCTION

It is comparatively easy for a manager to make a significant and direct impact on cost, and thus on profit, by cutting back on discretionary expenses or by changing the accounting policies adopted to allocate costs to accounting periods (e.g. Ferris, 1975; Griffiths, 1987). However, the latter practice has no real economic impact on the firm in terms of changing future cash flows as it involves merely 'book' accounting entries (unless it alters taxable profits and then the cost savings will have a negative effect). The former practice of reducing advertising, training, research and development, and capital expenditures does have an immediate and real effect. Costs are lowered and profits boosted. This effect occurs in the short-term, but there will also be other contrasting longer-term adverse effects on performance as sales drop off due to lack of new products, as lack of promotion of existing products results in falling sales and as product or service quality deteriorates due to a lack of skilled staff and suitable equipment. Expedient short-termism of this type can, therefore, undermine the competitiveness of a business and can threaten the longer-term well-being of the organization.

A policy of systematically managing costs on a continuous basis provides an alternative for management which can bring more stability, strength and growth potential to a business.

This will involve the regular provision of information designed to direct managerial attention to ways in which cost-effectiveness can be improved. It is an approach which will involve monitoring the full economic impact of the business, on resource acquisition and consumption. Nor should the process be one of response to crisis or one which is abandoned when the 'easy' cost improvements have been made. In Japan considerable resource is permanently allocated to this activity of cost management and the Japanese revisit the same products and areas of the business regularly. Japanese management accountants have a saying which emphasizes their commitment and determination.

Cost management is like wringing out a wet towel. The biggest reaction is obtained first, but we must keep wringing. Even when the towel appears dry to the touch we must wring it to extract more.

Achieving this level of effort and success in cost management requires the commitment of resources, the formulation and application of appropriate policies and procedures, and the establishment of a flow of relevant cost-based information. These topics, particularly the latter, are the subject matter of this book.

COST

Organizations are formed in order to attain certain objectives. However, the pursuit of these aims, be they economic, social or environmental, require a commitment of resources and the incurrence of cost. This is a book about cost. It is concerned with how costs can best be identified, measured, analysed, controlled and managed. As a starting point, however, cost must first be defined. The typical dictionary definition is straightforward.

What is or would have to be laid out or suffered or lost to obtain anything.

This definition closely reflects the view normally taken of cost by accountants in the business world. It is the cash outlays, owed or paid, which form the basis of the routine measurement of cost within a firm. These outlays can be derived from a transaction reference source (the purchase) which will also provide readily available documentation to validate the purchase price as the basis of cost measurement. This approach to costing has the attributes of convenience and practicality, and has the support of the accounting profession. For example, the Chartered Institute of Management Accountant's Official Terminology defines cost as:

(1) (as a noun). The amount of expenditure (actual or notional) incurred on, or attributable to, a specified thing or activity.
(2) (as a verb). To ascertain the cost of a specified thing or activity
   Note: The word cost can rarely stand alone and should be qualified as to its nature and limitations.

This definition highlights (in the note) that cost is usually qualified by reference to a particular object. The attribution of cost to a range of alternative objects has traditionally been the 'bread and butter' work of the cost accountants and Chapter 3 reviews this type of costing.

However, although the acquisition price provides a basis for practical costing systems it is not the only means of measuring cost. The economist views cost in terms of the latter part of the above dictionary definition, i.e. as what has been "lost to obtain anything". Cost, from this perspective, represents the benefits foregone from the best alternative opportunity when resources are committed to a particular course of action. Consequently the term 'opportunity cost' is applied to this approach. In the theory of the firm economists have operationalized the concept by including in costs a normal return on capital invested. This charge is intended to reflect the alternative investment possibilities, and provided the returns are positive (after taking account of this notional cost) then the firm's investment has been worthwhile. Accountants have applied this notion in the measurement of divisional performance where residual income represents a measure of profit achieved only after covering the cost of the capital. However, this does not provide a basis for measuring opportunity costs in all of the decision situations which confront a firm's management on a day to day basis. For example, the purchase of certain material may preclude the next best alternative use for the cash of hiring some new staff. The potential impact of the latter course of action on the worth of the business gives a measure of the opportunity cost of the material. However, after the cash has been committed to the material the opportunity cost changes. It will then be based on a consideration of the alternative uses to which the material can be put, including simply its resale. Clearly, opportunity cost is the type of cost information most relevant to decision situations but it is also a dynamic concept, changing over time as new opportunities come into being and existing ones disappear. It also involves some measure of subjectivity as it requires estimation of the future financial implications of the options which face the decision maker. For these reasons it does not provide a practical basis for the regular and routine measure of cost by accountants. However, it does provide an appropriate way of thinking about decision situations which highlights the limitations of the more conventional cost information based on acquisition prices.

THE PROCESS OF COST INCURRENCE

If cost incurrence is to be fully understood it should be viewed not simply as an event occurring at one point in time but as a process involving several stages. An understanding of the process is a prerequisite for the management of costs, as such knowledge is necessary to appreciate the nature of and behaviour of costs and to identify how and why costs have been incurred. Figure 2.1 provides an outline of the main stages in the process of cost incurrence and each is discussed in turn below.

Stage 1: Cost planning

Cost planning is a part of the basic planning activity of an organization. It will focus on the identification and specifica-

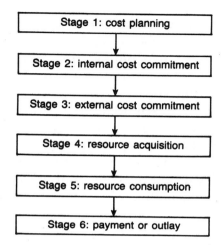

Figure 2.1 The process of cost incurrence.

tion of the resources required in order to achieve organizational aims. It will be based upon the generation of information and alternative options available for achieving these aims. Assessment will be made of internally available capacities and capabilities, and information on external resources which might be acquired will also be gathered. The choice between alternative courses of action will require a clear investigation of the cost implications of each before any commit-

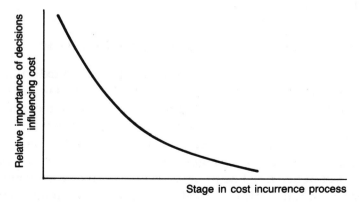

Figure 2.2 The cost commitment process.

ment is made. This stage therefore requires a major input of effort by the accountant to ensure cost-effectiveness is subsequently achieved when outlays are actually being made. Most of the important decisions effectively determining future costs are made at this stage (Figure 2.2). However, it has been suggested that the Western accountant's involvement is often small or non-existent at this stage. In contrast, in Japan it is recognized that at this stage costs can be significantly influenced and a major part of the accounting input occurs here (Brimson, 1986). Much of the content of this book is concerned with means by which the accountant can contribute at this stage.

Stage 2: Internal cost commitment

This stage is based on decisions being made within an organization on specific courses of action. It will involve the formalization of plans through documentation and authorization procedures. A detailed financial evaluation of the chosen plan will normally be available. In addition, top management approval and support will have shown their commitment to particular policies. Thus, although planned cost incurrence is approved and supported it is only at an internal level and reversal is still within the control of internal management.

Stage 3: External cost commitment

At this stage a link has been established with an external supplier of resources for the organization. This may take the form of an order being placed with a material supplier, a contract of employment being agreed with an employee or a contract signed for the supply of capital equipment. Reversal of an internal decision is no longer enough to stop the cost incurrence. Reference must be made to another party and, especially where a formal contractual relationship exists, some financial penalties may result.

Stage 4: Resource acquisition

This involves the physical receipt of the resource which has been acquired and only from this stage does the opportunity exist to apply the resource to the benefit.

Stage 5: Resource consumption

Resources acquired and used by organizations will fall into several different categories in respect of the way in which they are consumed by an organization.

Stockable resources

These comprise physical supplies, primarily materials or component parts which subsequent to acquisition may be held before use. Normally the full cost of this resource in terms of outlay has been incurred through acquisition. Therefore, prompt use and recovery through sale is financially desirable (hence the attraction, for example, of JIT stocking policies). Cessation of use should promptly impact on acquisition and cash outlay but can result in the need for stock disposals.

Time-related resources

These comprise service potentials acquired for a period of time, and cost is therefore clocked up by the passage of time. Examples include salaried (as opposed to piece-rate) employees, rentals (both equipment and building) and periodic local rates. The availability of the resource for a period of time is obtained in return for the cash outlay and appropriateness, and intensity of its use during that period is then a matter for management. Cessation of use during the period will not be mirrored in an immediate elimination of the outlay.

Capital resources

These comprise purchased capital equipment. Here the outlay will occur around the time of acquisition and this forms the basis of the cost to the organization. However, equipment will normally be used or consumed by an organization over several years. To reflect this the acquisition cost is allocated in appropriate portions to each of these years. This annual charge is termed depreciation and although it should reflect asset consumption it is usually computed by a 'rule of thumb', such as an equal apportionment to each year of asset life. The disposal of a piece of equipment will result in the elimination of the related depreciation charge but this will have no effect on the cash outlays of the firm.

'Consume as acquired' resources
These comprise resources where acquisition, consumption and frequently payment all occur at a similar time. Examples would include piece-work labour, power costs and other service charges for telephone usage, repair work, etc. Cessation of usage will have a direct and immediate impact on consumption and cash outlays.

Thus, where information is provided on the cost as reflecting resources consumed it must be remembered that the constituent of the cost will be different in nature, in particular an increase in, or indeed the elimination of the consumption, of each type of resource will be significantly different in its underlying economic impact on the organization's future cash flows.

Stage 6: Payment or outlay

This last stage reflects the real economic impact on an organization in terms of its cash flow. In practice it may be delayed as long as practicable and, for example, for many supermarkets it will in fact occur after goods supplied have been sold. The financial benefits of delay must also be weighed against the benefits of maintaining a good relationship with suppliers. Where prompt payment is made this stage may in fact precede at least stage 5.

Thus, the management of cost incurrence involves the management of a process, not simply of an event. Due to the different nature of resources acquired and consumed by organizations, reported costs may be of different economic significance. For example, where the cost stems from prior capital expenditure on equipment its avoidance, perhaps by dropping the product which uses that equipment, will not produce a similar cash saving. In other words, costs which reflect consumption of resources do not mirror directly their cash flow impact. This distinction is highlighted by Cooper and Kaplan (1991) and should be a prime consideration of uses of cost information.

COSTS IN FINANCIAL STATEMENTS

While cost information for decision making should focus upon the future cash flow implications of alternative actions, managers will also be concerned about how cost incurrence impinges on their performance as reported to the organization's owners. This has traditionally been achieved through the publication of two financial statements: the balance sheet and the profit and loss account. These statements are prepared by applying three fundamental accounting principles: conservatism,

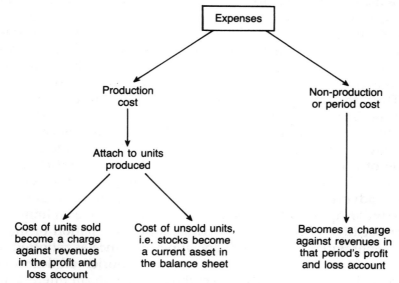

Figure 2.3 Costs and financial statements.

accruals and matching. Each of these principles influences the determination of costs in the financial statements. Conservatism ensures that profits are not overstated and this requires the prompt recognition of all costs. Accruals ensure that credit transactions are included when revenues and expenditures are recognized. Matching concerns the selection of appropriate revenues and costs for the determination of profit for a particular period of time. The application of these principles prescribes a particular view of reported costs. Figure 2.3 outlines this view.

Expenses are first classified as to whether or not they relate to production, i.e. those relating to incurrence,

. . . bring the product or service to its present location and condition. This expenditure should include, in addition to cost of purchase, such costs of conversion as were appropriate to that location and condition.

The organization's product costing system will then attach these production costs to units produced, the cost of those units sold becoming a charge (cost of sales) which is matched against sales revenue to determine gross profit. In contrast, the production cost of unsold units will be treated as the current asset stock in the balance sheet. Non-production expenses, such as general management and sales and distribution, are treated as period costs being charged directly to the profit and loss account in the period in which they are incurred.

Thus, the outlay of funds may have a very different impact on the financial performance of an organization, particularly in the short-term. Profit may be reduced immediately by the outlay (e.g. period costs) or with a lag to reflect production and sale of products (production costs). Often the benefits of the former class of cost will only be forthcoming in future periods (e.g. advertising and research and development). Moreover, the build-up of cost in unsold stocks will not have an immediate negative effect on profit. Thus, a pre-occupation of management with short-term financial performance as reflected in the profit and loss account can lead to cost-oriented decisions which do not necessarily reflect the best long-term interests of the organization.

COST MANAGEMENT

Cost management involves initiating and making decisions which will improve the cost-effectiveness of an organization. In order to achieve this managers have to understand the concepts of cost discussed above within the context of their own business. They must have a basic knowledge of the factors which influence or drive costs and appreciate the extent or power of each factor. They must know how their decisions can change costs and be alerted to situations where costs require changing and/or the opportunity to beneficially alter costs exists. This requires the provision of a regular flow of reliable and relevant cost information which can be clearly communicated to the relevant individuals. This information should relate costs both to cause and to the purpose of its incurrence, i.e. managers should know how costs have been incurred and also what objectives they have been incurred to support.

Cost management activity should be continuous and should be an integrated activity throughout the whole life cycle of an organization's products or services. For example, it is at the pre-production stages that cost management activity can have its biggest impact as so many of the decisions leading to cost commitments are only being considered at this time. The planning and design of a new product should only be complete when estimated cost targets have been satisfactorily met.

To be effective, cost management has to be accepted as a policy by company management. They must set the correct environment and provide the resources for it to flourish. In Japan a number of pre-conditions are generally accepted as a basis for cost management. These are outlined in Table 2.1 and emphasize the need to provide useful cost information at the time when the important decisions influencing cost are taken. In recent years, both in the West and in Japan, a series of techniques have emerged to support this type of cost management activity. They involve both changes in the way cost information is generated and in the way it is attributed for use by managers. This book brings these techniques together for the first time.

Table 2.1 Pre-conditions for cost management

1. Product plans which are both timely and effective in cost terms are a key foundation of profitability.
2. The source of profit is not the physical effort involved in production and selling but the intellectual effort in planning and designing the production and sales processes. Those involved in intellectual work should not be diverted from it by other responsibilities. Line managers and workers are there to realize the plans created by the intellectual efforts of others.
3. Managing the intellectual effort should focus not on improving efficiency but in achieving effectiveness in product specification. Great effort is required; the designers slogan should be 'your next specification is God'.
4. Cost is not simply incurred, it should reflect only **purposeful** spending. Any spending should be able to be linked to the generation of profit.
5. Cost information should be generated to show the sources of profit. Thus, from point 2 above, cost accounting should focus at the intellectual activity stage. The fixing of a product specification removes most of the ability to alter costs.
6. Appropriate cost information and expertise must be available at all pre-production stages and design should have target cost achievement as an objective.

REFERENCES

Brimson, J.A. (1986) How advanced technologies are reshaping cost management. *Management Accounting (US)*, March, **67**, 25–9.

Cooper, R. and Kaplan, R.S. (1991) Profit priorities from activity based costing. *Harvard Business Review*, May–June, **69**.

Ferris, K.R. (1975) Profit forecast disclosure: the effect on managerial behaviour. *Accounting and Business Research*, Spring, **5**, 133–9.

Griffiths, I. (1987) *Creative Accounting*, Unwin Hyman, London.

CHAPTER THREE

Conventional cost analysis

INTRODUCTION

The purpose of practical management accounting information have been neatly summarized by March and Simon (1958) in an enduring manner based on their analysis of the role of accounting within business organizations. They comprise three broad areas:

(1) to direct attention, i.e. to alert management to the need to consider particular aspects of the organization's performance and if possible to guide action in respect of the issue which has arisen;
(2) to assist in problem solving, i.e. to provide information of relevance to decisions facing management;
(3) to 'scorekeep', i.e. to show how the organization has been doing through the measurement of its performance.

These three purposes also underlie the approaches which accountants have traditionally adopted in the analysis of cost. This chapter examines accounting practice in this respect by focusing on the four bases of cost analysis which comprise the foundations of conventional cost accounting: classificational (by type), relational (by cost object), behavioural (by the way in which cost varies, and temporal (in relation to time). Each may be considered a different dimension from which cost may be viewed. For clarity and convenience they are considered individually. However, in practice the cost information produced by accountants will frequently combine ideas from more than one of these types of analysis. For example, standard costs incorporate both a temporal dimension (being future oriented) and a relational dimension (being based on a unit of output). This chapter therefore provides a description of conventional practice and an assesment of how well the above purposes can be served by it in a contemporary business environment. This analysis provides a basis for the subsequent suggestions of approaches which can contribute to the development of an improved and modern approach to cost management.

ACCOUNTING COST ANALYSIS

Classificational

In order to facilitate the capture, recording and reporting of costs from the large volume of individual purchase transactions in which an organization will engage, the accountant will categorize them and then collect and aggregate data on them under these categories. This categorization is conventionally based on the nature of what is acquired when an outlay is made. For example, the transaction for various types of materials for use in production, wages paid to various grades of labour and the cost of bought in services, such as power, heat, rent and insurance, are analysed into separate accounts in the book-keeping system so that periodic totals for each can be obtained readily. This is a basic form of analysis which shows what an organization's money has been spent on. It provides an inventory of inputs to the system, i.e. the types of resources acquired and the price paid for them. This information is normally used directly in the internal profit and loss account where the costs are listed and matched with revenue to show whether a profit or loss has been made.

Accountants will also frequently summarize this information further into four major categories of cost (Figure 3.1). First, direct material which represents the cost of materials directly traceable to the product or service. Second, direct labour which represents the cost of production workers time directly traceable to the production or services. Third, the production overhead which comprises an array of costs which are incurred to support a wide range of production activity, e.g. supervision, quality control, occupancy costs. The term 'overhead' is applied as it is incurred for several products or services and cannot be directly linked to any particular one. Fourth, the non-production overhead which comprises selling and distribution and administration and general management costs. The first two categories together are referred to as direct or prime costs, the first three as production costs and the fourth as period costs (being primarily considered a cost of the time period in which they are incurred). All four together give the total cost.

Conventionally this is the basic type of cost information which will be available in most organizations. Its use in preparing the profit and loss account indicates a value in assessing the stewardship of management as this type of cost analysis shows how funds have been dispersed during a given period.

Individual transactions	Cost types	Cost classification
Material purchases	Material A Material B Material C	Direct material
Wages payments	Production wages (process) Production wages (grinding) Production wages (assembly)	Direct labour
Production overhead payments	Factory rent and rates Machine maintenance Machine insurance Factory electricity Factory supervision	Production overhead
Sales cost payments	Salesperson's salaries Advertising Distribution transport General management salaries	Non-production overhead

Figure 3.1 Cost classification.

By monitoring it over time, changes and trends can be observed in the input side of the process. It also provides an indication of the basic cost structure of an organization which can be used as a basis for comparison with other, normally competing, organizations. To analyse what has been done with the acquired resources and to link them to the outputs of the organization requires an extension of cost information beyond mere classification by type. However, its focus is on the input side of the organization as it simply provides a description of the costs of resources.

Relational

The value of cost information for management is usually enhanced by relating it to a cost object. This practice may take many forms as a whole range of cost objects can be used. Traditionally the most common are products and organizational subunits, such as departments and divisions. The former can, when linked with product volume information, also be used as a basis for segmenting costs in relation to market segments so that sources of profitability can be identified. In addition, it provides a basis for stock valuation, decision making (e.g. prices and outputs), control (e.g. where the cost information represents targets for achievement as in standard cost) and performance assessment (e.g. where a manager has responsibility for all aspects of individual products). Figures 3.2 and 3.3 show how information is collected on product cost using, respectively, job costing, where each unit of output is unique and has to be costed individually, and process costing, where continuous runs of identical product units are manufactured. The latter two cost objects are primarily geared to the assessment and control of performance as they frequently match areas of individual managerial authority. They can therefore contribute to the operation of a system of responsibility accounting in which the actual costs are matched against target or budgeted costs. In addition, departmental cost information is a prerequisite for the conventional approaches to product costing where production overhead rates are normally based on production departments.

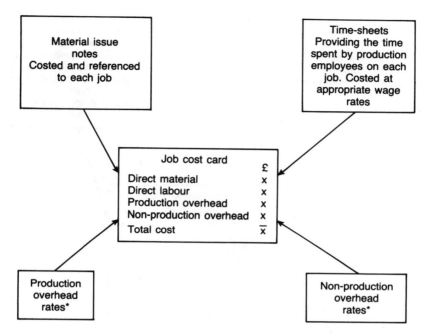

Figure 3.2 Job costing.* Overhead rates are normally based on pre-determined or estimated figures so that the rate to be used is available throughout the relevant period.

The carving up of cost among cost objects is one of the more problematic areas of accounting, for while some costs can be clearly and conveniently related to a cost object others cannot. Consequently the end result is based to some extent on subjective and somewhat arbitrary procedures which limit the accuracy and utility of the end result. For example, in product costing the attachment of production overhead costs is problematic as these types of costs are common to several products. The rent of a factory used to produce several product lines exemplifies the situation. Conventionally, a three-stage procedure will be involved in its unitization (Figure 3.4).

In Stage 1 the rent is apportioned to all the departments in the factory. This may be done on the basis of the relative floor areas of each department. In Stage 2 the cost of the two service departments (machine maintenance and canteen) are re-appor-

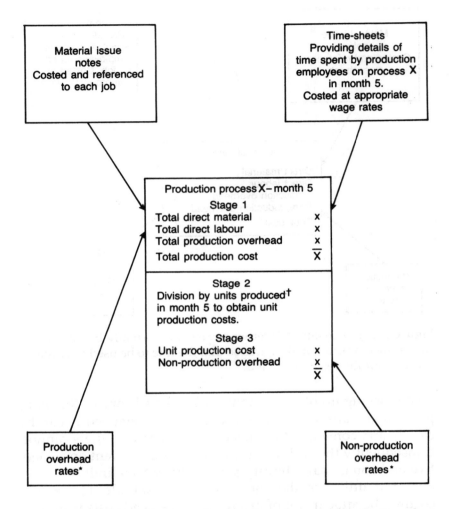

Figure 3.3 Process costing.* Overhead rates are normally based on pre-determined or estimated figures so that the rate to be used is available throughout the relevant period.† Although good finished units of output are identical in any production period production output units will lack homogeneity due to the existence of substandard units (process losses) and work in process both at the start and end of the period. To obtain a common denominator for division in these situations the concept of equivalent units is applied. This is explained in detail in standard management accounting texts.

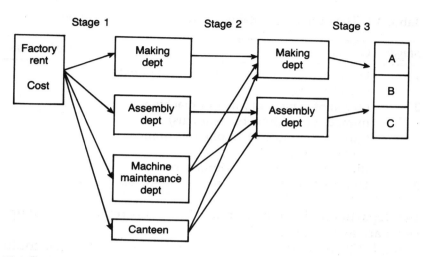

Figure 3.4 Cost flows in unitizing overheads.

tioned to the two mainstream production departments (making and assembly). This may be done, respectively, on the basis of number of machines and number of employees. Finally, the resultant rent cost in making and assembly is attached to individual products through the use of overhead rates obtained by dividing the overhead cost of the department by a production characteristic which ideally has a close causal relationship to the incurrence of the overhead cost. As rent is a time-related cost then direct labour hours might be used. Application of such a rate means that the rent cost would be shared out among products in proportion to the direct labour hours worked on each. If one re-examines the above decisions at each stage the arbitrariness becomes apparent. In Stage 1 volume rather than floor area might be viewed as a basis for apportionment. Some weighting for the inbuilt fittings in each area might also be appropriate. In Stage 2 the number of machine breakdowns and number of canteen visits might be alternative bases for reappointment of the service departments. The existence of reciprocal services between the two service departments might also be recognized at this stage. Finally, machine hours rather than labour hours might be used as the basis for

Table 3.1 The option's available at each stage of utilization

Stage	Options	No. of options
1	Floor area or volume with each weighted to reflect fittings	4
2	(a) Maintenance (number of machines, number of machine breakdowns) Canteen (number of employees, number of canteen visits)	4
	(b) Consideration of reciprocal services	2
3	Direct labour hours or machine hours basis	4

the departmental overhead rates. From this review several options are available at each stage (Table 3.1).

In all, 128 alternative product costs ($4 \times 4 \times 2 \times 4 = 128$) could be obtained using various permutations of the options in Table 3.1. In reality the number of options at each stage is considerably greater than those outlined in Table 3.1. Moreover, the analysis in Table 3.1 applies to a single cost when in practice overheads will be numerous. Thus, in an organization of any complexity with substantial overheads unit cost information will only represent **one** possible cost from among many. The product cost is merely a chimera.

A similar difficulty arises where costs incurred centrally are allocated to the divisions of a business. For example, group advertising might be allocated on the basis of divisional sales. This practice would pose several problems for the user of the resultant information. First, the resultant divisional cost allocation would not be controllable at divisional level. Second, sales growth would be penalized as it would attract a higher cost allocation. Third, the performance of divisions would become interdependent with a fall in sales in one division causing the remaining divisions to be burdened with a higher cost allocation. For these reasons the value of, say, divisional profit statements incorporating allocated costs will be questionable, as performance is a function of accounting procedures as well as operational considerations.

However, there are several benefits also cited for making such cost allocations. They make divisional managers aware of the existence of these costs and therefore may stimulate them to press for their containment and reduction. At the level of product cost they may be a necessity, required for stock valuation by accounting standard or for pricing purposes on Government contracts. Where cost plus pricing is used then, once again, a full unit cost will have to be computed.

Relating cost to a range of cost objects is one of the main activities of the management accountant. If the end result is to provide useful information then the procedures adopted must be tailored to suit the information's end purpose. Information gathered for one purpose (e.g. unit cost for stock valuation) may not be appropriate for another (the product mix decision). However, it is often general and incorrect use of available information in this way which leads to criticism of management accounting. In addition, an awareness of the limitations of the procedures underlying the generation of relational cost information is necessary if it is to be used with due care. The ability to directly charge cost to cost objects rather than apply subjective allocations is a desirable development and one which is becoming more prevalent in practice.

Behavioural

Underlying a sound ability to understand and explain cost is a knowledge of how the costs of an organization have behaved in the past and are expected to behave in the future. This type of analysis is conventionally undertaken in respect of the major factor influencing total cost incurrence, i.e. production volume. When costs are related to this variable a variety of patterns are usually apparent (Figure 3.5).

In essence, costs either vary in some way with volume or they do not. In reality much of the variation is probably non-linear but linearity is assumed as a simplification. Moreover, a simple dual categorization of costs as either fixed (no variation with volume) or variable (linear variations with volume) is usually made as a further simplification. This segregation may be achieved by the subjective judgement of accountants and managers. Alternatively, it can be done in a more refined manner

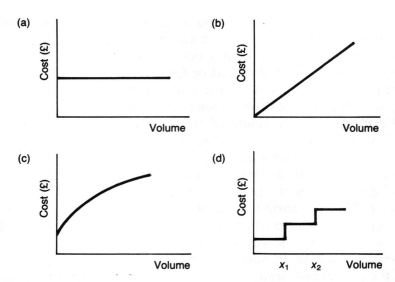

Figure 3.5 Variations in cost behaviour with respect to production volume. (a) Fixed cost, e.g. factory rent; (b) variable cost, e.g. Royalty payment permit; (c) semi-variable cost, e.g. power for production and heat and light; (d) semi-fixed cost, e.g. machine depreciation where new machines are installed at x_1 and x_2.

by regression analysis where suitable data are available to carry out the requisite statistical analysis. Even this approach will be limited by the existence of non-volume factors affecting the data, e.g. inflation or changes in technology. However, once the split is achieved the user of the resultant information should bear in mind that it is an abstraction from a whole series of more complex relationships and cannot be 100% accurate. The results of analyses conducted using merely the two categories of cost – fixed and variable – will therefore best be handled with some sensitivity in respect of the basic data. The common separation of cost is as follows:

	direct material
Variable cost	direct labour
	variable production overhead
Fixed cost	fixed production overhead

Where the analysis calls for it, non-production and overheads would also be divided between the two categories.

The first area of use for this type of cost analysis is in profit measurement. Here, instead of the conventional use of full unit cost to value stocks and work in progress in the computation of the cost of sales figure, only the variable cost will be used. The resultant profit and loss account differs from the conventional one and is shown in Table 3.2.

Table 3.2 Full cost and variable cost-based profit and loss account (in £)

Full cost basis			
	Sales		x
	Stock start (at full production cost)	x	
plus	Cost of production (at full production cost)	(x)	
		x	
less	Stock (end) (at full production cost)	(x)	
	Cost of sales (at full production cost)		(x)
	Gross profit		x
	Non-production overheads		(x)
	Net profit		(x)
variable cost basis			
	Sales		x
	Stock start (at variable production cost)	x	
plus	Cost of production (at variable production cost)	(x)	
		x	
less	Stock (end) (at variable production cost)	(x)	
		x	
	Non-production variable overheads	(x)	
	Variable cost of sales		(x)
	Contribution		x
	Fixed production overheads	x	
	Fixed non-production overheads	(x)	(x)
	Net profit		(x)

The variable cost basis of profit measurement has several notable advantages. First, it avoids the need for the arbitrary allocations involved in unitizing fixed overheads in order to obtain a full unit cost. Second, it may be viewed as a prudent means of profit measurement as it ensures that all fixed costs are written off in the profit and loss account in the period of their incurrence. None are carried forward as a part of the asset stock. As fixed costs may often be viewed as providing the capacity to produce primarily in a period of time (e.g. rent, insurance, rates, etc.) then this treatment may be deemed appropriate, as it matches cost to time period and does not permit the carry forward (in stock) of any of the cost of unused capacity. Third, the measure of contribution (sales less variable cost of sales) being devoid of the influence of fixed costs provides a basis for the assessment of volume changes on profitability. For example, accountants will normally assume (within a relevant range) that a 5% increase in sales volume will also result in a 5% boost to contribution and profits. Thus, profits measured in this way closely reflect changes in sales volume and as profits are realized only on sales this may be viewed as a desirable relationship to reflect in the profit and loss account. In contrast, a full cost basis of stock valuation allows production volumes, through their impact on stock levels, to affect the cost of sales and hence profit figures. For example, a stock build-up can actually improve profits as the fixed costs attaching to it are treated as part of the stock asset rather than being charged to the profit and loss account. Moreover when contribution is applied to individual products (or segments of the business) it provides a view of the impact on overall profitability of that particular product (or segment) undistorted by arbitrary fixed cost allocations.

The identification of product variable unit cost is also an important ingredient in the provision of information for output decisions. By applying it to volume changes the cost implications of product mix, product line cessation and make or buy decisions can all be estimated. In addition, at the stage of planning future profitability the availability of information on unit variable costs and fixed costs will allow the construction of break-even models. These models can contribute to the planning process by showing how profit will change as sales volume alters. As shown in Figure 3.6, the profit can be readily forecast at different volume levels and the resultant margin of safety (i.e. extent to which output exceeds the break-even level) identified.

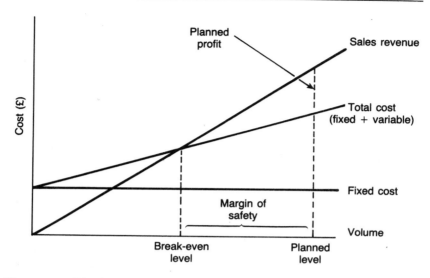

Figure 3.6 The basic break-even model.

The above analysis is clear and easy to present but is based on a whole range of simplistic assumptions, including the ability to fully separate fixed and variable costs, the linearity of both costs and revenues with respect to volume, the non-existence of stocks and that the sales mix is constant. It therefore provides a 'rule of thumb' approach to planning which will provide reasonable realism, at best, only over a very restricted range of output.

One other application of the contribution notion lies in the area of control. This relates to its use as a basis for measuring volume variances in economic terms. For example, if actual sales output falls short of budgeted sales then an unfavourable volume variance exits. Multiplying the number of units shortfall by the expected unit contribution would provide a measure of the variance in terms of the profit lost. Known as a sales contribution margin variance, this provides feedback to management on the economic impact of factors affecting sales volume. However, the assumption of cost and revenue linearity with respect to output volume still underlies this practice.

All of the above analyses require the identification of costs as fixed or variable. This involves the categorization of many grey areas as black or white. For example, direct labour costs are almost always treated as variable, more productive labour being required when production increases and less when it is reduced. This virtually presupposes that direct labour is paid by results on a piece-work basis rather than by a fixed periodic salary, and that labour resources can, in fact, be readily dispensed with when output falls. The payment of time-based salaries and the existence of employment laws and corporate polices of no compulsory redundancies may make these assumptions unrealistic. As shown in Chapter 1, cost incurrence and reduction involves a process which takes time. Instead of simply using a unit variable cost to explain cost variations in relation to volume changes, Shillinglaw (1968) has suggested the use of the concept of attributable cost in order to overcome these difficulties. As the name suggests, this involves a specific identification in any decision situation involving a reduction in output of the costs which will no longer be incurred. In practice these will often exclude several of the costs conventionally classified as variable by management accountants. While it certainly provides one area which should be explored when the figures underlying a decision analysis are being considered, it does require individual assessment of the decision situation.

Finally, it should be borne in mind that cost behaviour will not simply be a function of production volume. Miller and Vollmann (1985) have highlighted this fact by emphasizing the importance of transactions relating to the logistics, balancing change and quality of manufacturing operations as drivers of overhead cost. These transactions relate to the complexity and diversity of production rather than purely its volume but they still have a major impact on overhead in contemporary manufacturing operations. The development of activity-based costing (Chapters 8 and 9) is one recent development aimed at dealing with this situation.

Temporal

Acquisition cost is set in a particular time frame, i.e. the date of purchase of the relevant resource. It therefore quickly becomes an historic cost, a reflection of a past transaction. This limits the utility of this type of cost information in two ways. First, from a decision-maker's point of view, it is regarded as a sunk cost. The financial information relevant to a decision comprises the future differential cash inflows and outflows caused by the decision action. These, of course, require estimation and in this respect historic acquisition costs may prove useful, by providing a basis for the necessary estimates. Although sunk costs may be irrelevant to decisions from a purely financial perspective they do represent a residue from past decisions and evidence commitments. They may therefore have a behavioural impact on decision makers whose current and past performance may be reflected in them. Second, the existence of inflation will reduce the current relevance of historic costs as time passes. The replacement of resources previously acquired will require outlays which differ in both money amount and purchasing power from the original acquisition price. Thus, if cost information is expected to reflect current conditions then the contemporary prices of equivalent resources may be monitored so that a replacement cost is known. This will provide an indication of the sacrifice being made in using resources which the organization will have to replace if it is to function as a going concern. For example, if sale price does not cover the current replacement cost of resources consumed then the organization will have to shrink the size of its operations or obtain additional non-trading funding.

The management accountant will also produce information on future costs. These will often be components of a master budget and classified therein by cost element and type. The derivation of these future costs may take various forms from the addition of an inflation 'allowance' to previous year figures, to a zero-based approach where all budget costs have to be rejustified each year, or a priority-based approach, where future resource consumption is ranked in order of importance in relation to the organization's aims (e.g. Bhada and Minimier, 1980). Expected future costs may also be unitized and the resultant cost, termed a standard cost, may be used as a target for cost efficiency. It will provide a measure of the expected resources consumed by a unit of each product – the price which should be paid for these resources. A basis is therefore provided for the ascertainment of the master budget's direct costs (through multiplication by production volumes). In addition, a whole series of variance computations can be made from a comparison with actual performance. Conventionally these relate to both the use of (efficiency) and payment for (price) each element of cost. In so doing they support the operation of a system of responsibility accounting. Moreover, the generation of future or budgeted costs provides a focus for the planning function and they give a context within which actual performance can be framed and some measure of control achieved. Table 3.3 illustrates the type of report which can be produced from an integrated standard costing system. The detail provided allows more interpretation of the performance. For example, the following questions may be raised.

(1) Did the charging of higher selling prices cause a fall off in the volume demanded?
(2) Did the lower price paid for materials represent good buying or the acquisition of poorer quality supplies? (The unfavourable usage variance hints at the latter.)
(3) Are lower grades of labour being used and is this causing the deterioration in efficiency.
(4) Why are we producing more than our budget when sales volume is down on budget?

Finally, when unitized as standard costs with the fixed and variable elements identified they provide a necessary ingredient for the output volume decisions described earlier in this chapter.

Time is also an important consideration when cost behaviour or variability is to be considered. Cost variability changes with the time span perspective which is taken. The economist views costs from both a short- and long-term perspective. The former is based on the assumption that the capital equipment of the organization must be taken as given and only direct labour, direct materials and bought-in services can be varied. The lat-

Table 3.3 Variance report for January 19XX[a]

	£'000s	£'000s
Budgeted sales		2000
Sales variances		
Sales volume	90U [b]	
Sales price	20F [c]	70U
Actual sales		1930
less standard cost of actual sales		1500
Standard profit		430 [d]
Cost variances		
Direct material: price	40F [e]	
usage	60U [f]	
Direct labour: rate	20U [g]	
efficiency	30U [h]	
Variable overhead: spending	10F [i]	
efficiency	20U [j]	
Fixed overhead: spending	20F [k]	
volume	50F [l]	10U
Profit		420

[a] U, unfavourable; F, favourable.
[b] Indicates less units than expected were sold.
[c] Indicates higher sales prices than expected were achieved.
[d] What profit would have been had costs been as expected.
[e] Indicates a lower price was paid for materials than expected.
[f] Indicates more materials were used than expected at our actual level of production.
[g] Production workers were paid a higher wage rate than expected.
[h] Production workers took longer to produce our actual output than expected.
[i] Lower prices were obtained for variable overheads than expected.
[j] Longer working than expected (see [h]) has caused higher variable overhead cost.
[k] Lower prices were obtained for fixed overheads than expected.
[l] More units were produced than expected when setting the original budget for January.

ter perspective assumes that time is available to change the plant and equipment available. In their approach to decision analysis, accountants have tended to pursue the former approach using direct material, direct labour and variable overhead as their proxy for short-term variable cost. This information is then applied to decisions involving both product output levels and product range. However, particularly in the case of the latter decision, a strategic and medium- to long-term dimension is certainly apparent and criticisms have been made (Kaplan, 1990) of the inappropriate use of short-term costs in these situations. The incorporation of costs which can vary over the longer-term is the most suitable product cost information for this purpose (Johnson and Kaplan, 1987).

Finally, costs and time are related by the time value of money. Other things being equal it is better to pay the same amount of money for something (which one has obtained) in the future rather than today. Thus, in assessing the sacrifice which a future cost will involve for an organization an outlay should be discounted to its present value. This involves using a rate which reflects the organization's time preference for money (usually its cost of capital). Similarly, cost savings involving the avoidance of future cash outlays can be adjusted for the timing of their occurrence in the same way. Particularly where comparisons are being made between options which involve different cost patterns then the expression of costs versus benefits in present value terms allows them to be matched on a comparable basis and a **net** present value computed to provide a sound basis for judgement.

CONCLUSION

Analyses of the type described above have provided the basis for cost accounting systems for the past century or more. They clearly possess many attributes which have stood the test of time and will no doubt continue to contribute to many aspects of cost management in the future. However, they also have the limitations discussed above, and particularly in the context of a contemporary environment these are accentuated and can generate irrelevant, or worse, misleading information. Recognition of these limitations is the first step in developing a contemporary cost management system which will meet Robert Kaplan's (1983, p. 689) challenge to management accountants to:

. . . devise new internal accounting systems that will be supportive of the firm's new manufacturing strategy.

Since this challenge, several developments aimed at improving the quality of information have occurred in the area of cost management. They cover many of the areas where conventional practices show limitations. These are described and reviewed in the subsequent chapters. Together they provide the reader with the opportunity to explore and assess the various possibilities for developing and enhancing their cost management system in ways which will positively support the achievement of organizational goals.

REFERENCES

Bhada, Y.K. and Minimier, G. (1980) Integrate ZBB into your MBO Framework. *Financial Executive*, June, **48**, 42–7.

Johnson, H.T. and Kaplan, R.S. (1987) The importance of long-term product cost. *The McKinsey Quarterly*, Autumn, 36–48.

Kaplan, R.S. (1983) Measuring manufacturing Performance: a new challenge for management accounting research, *The Accounting Review*, October, **58**, 686–705.

Kaplan, R.S. (1990) Contribution margin analysis and the activity based approach. *Journal of Management Accounting Research*, Fall, **2**, 2–15.

March, J.G. and Simon, H.A. (1958) *Organisations*, Wiley, New York.

Miller, J.G. and Vollmann, T.E. (1985) The hidden factory. *Harvard Business Review*, September/October, **63**, 142–50.

Shillinglaw, G. (1968) The concept of attributable cost, in *Studies in Cost Analysis* (ed. D. Solomons), Sweet and Maxwell, London, pp. 134–47.

CHAPTER FOUR

Target cost management

DEFINITION OF TARGET COST MANAGEMENT

Various opinions have been expressed as to what target cost management (TCM) is at the product design stage. The origin of the concept of TCM can be found in cost engineering and cost management, but it is a dynamic growing concept and today more and more implementations and interpretations are being developed.

TCM is a management technology using scientific principles and technologies to establish a cost target, breakdown the cost target, and improve cost. TCM adopts these technologies through the development and design phases in order to achieve product specification cost within the cost targets that are included in the life cycle cost: development, design, manufacturing, distribution, sales, usage, and disposal costs. TCM can also be called a management methodology and technology tool to make new products at a 'reasonable cost' that should be achieved through product development and design activities to meet all the required target costs in the company.

OUTLINE OF TCM

The development of TCM has five stages: planning, concept design, basic design, detailed design, and manufacturing preparation. The necessary steps within each stage are outlined as follows.

Step 1: Product planning

New product planning is summarized in a document and/or table which defines and clarifies the design requirements. Usually, the following items for the new product are shown in the document and/or table:

(1) Outline of the mission and concept of the product.
(2) Primary performance specifications, and design schedule, manufacturing and marketing activities for the product.
(3) Cost target, selling price, sales volume and profitability study for the product.

Step 2: Concept design

At this stage, we formulate the basic concept, normal selling price and attainable cost target of the new product on the basis of the design requirements. Usually, this stage comprises the following items:

(1) Formulation of main function areas.
(2) Assignment of the cost target to the top level function areas.
(3) Designing the basic concept of the product under the assigned cost target.
(4) Ascertaining whether or not the basic concept of the product is designed to fit the cost target by using a rough cost estimation.
(5) A profitability study of the product.

Step 3: Basic design

The focus of this stage is to construct a general drawing of the product based on the cost target. In many cases, it is composed of the following items:

(1) Assignment of the cost target to the top and middle function areas or main components.
(2) Framing a general drawing under the cost target.
(3) Ascertaining whether or not the general drawing of the product is designed to fit the cost target by making use of the rough cost estimation.

Step 4: Detailed design

At this stage, we draw up the manufacturing specifications of the product on the basis of the framework of the general drawing and the cost target described in step 3. Usually, it is composed of the following items:

(1) Drawing up the details of design (manufacturing specification) under the cost target.
(2) Ascertaining whether or not the manufacturing specifications of the product are designed to fit the cost target by using a detailed cost estimation.

Step 5: Manufacturing preparation

At this stage, a manufacturing system and variations of the product are designed, manufacturing methods and processes of the product are determined under the cost target. The main activities and general flow chart of TCM are described in Figure 4.1. (Tanaka, 1992)

DESIGN TO COST

One important origin of target cost management is the 'design to cost' (DTC) approach adopted by the American Department of Defense (1975). The approach was developed to help in reducing the uncertainty of cost and improve cost control in an industry notorious for cost overruns. The basic idea behind design to cost is to establish a target cost for the planning, design and purchasing stages of a new product and to use this target cost to monitor and control the actual costs incurred. In design to cost, the target cost is set at the level which can be achieved with the greatest possible efforts from designers. In applying this approach, the American Department of Defense establishes not only product target costs but also target costs for areas such as maintenance and supply expenses. It is thus a technique focusing on the internal capabilities of an organization. Combining this approach with the complimentary external market-based target costs provides an excellent basis for cost management.

TARGET COST CONCEPTS

The target cost is the cost to be achieved during the planning, design and preparation for manufacturing stages of a new product and it therefore influences discussions about the product's nature and specification. However, it is a concept which can be viewed in two ways. First, there are the costs incurred by the manufacturer, such as planning and design costs, devel-

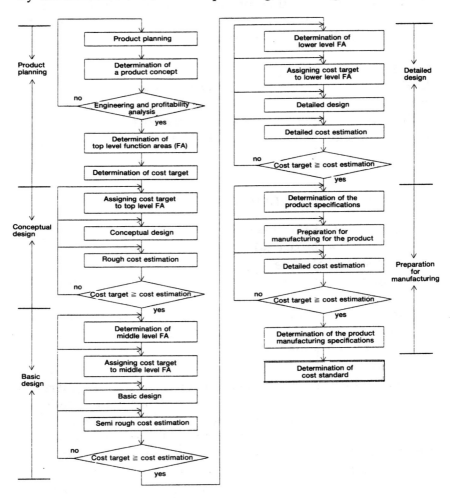

Figure 4.1 General flow chart of TCM.

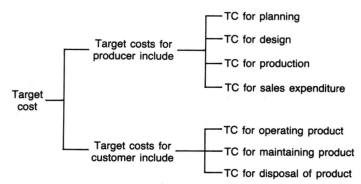

Figure 4.2 Different types of target cost.

opment, manufacturing and sales costs. Second, there are the costs incurred by the customer for the product, such as maintenance, operating and disposal costs (Tanaka, 1988). In current practice target cost usually concentrates on the manufacturer's costs but in the future, if a product life cycle viewpoint is taken, target cost could well be developed to include the costs incurred both by the manufacturer and the customer as both types of cost are relevant to the competitive success of a product (Figure 4.2). Another dimension of target costing which may vary in practice is the type of target to be set. This can vary from the tight and difficult to achieve (Newbrough, 1967) to the practical reflecting recent experience (Heyel, 1982). While prevailing market conditions may be a predominant influence on this issue there may also be scope to modify the target to the type which will have the best motivational effect in the situation in which it is being used.

It would also be misleading to give the impression that there is a standard focus for a target cost as various cost objects can be used for the target. For example, departments or activities might be used and costs controlled in relation to a cost object based on the functions of the product or the parts of the product (see Chapter 5). This can be done to aid in the cost reduction process by pinpointing where effort can be fruitful. The degree of segmentation can be varied considerably. Increasing detail can help to guide action while an overall approach leaves scope for more flexibility in the approaches adopted to meet the target. If target costing is to be effective it should motivate the planners and designers and producers of products. If the target cost is too severe they may lose their motivation and give up. If the target cost is set so that it can be attained easily, again this may not motivate the planners and designers. The degree of detail and the focus of the target will also be pertinent to their motivation. In terms of behavioural implications, setting a target cost is as much an art as a science; organizations must learn from experimentation and experience, as the exact approach adopted will be influenced situationally.

A further area of variation in target costing involves setting a target with tolerance limits. In other words, a target cost band rather than a single target figure is used. Tolerance limits may also be set between cost and performance, cost and specification, and cost and date of delivery.

FACTORS INVOLVED IN SETTING TARGET COSTS

When setting a target cost, two sets of factors must be taken into consideration: general management considerations and specific product and situational considerations.

General management considerations

First, before starting to set a target cost, the scope of the target cost must be defined. For example, which of the following costs should it include: planning and design stages of a new product; manufacturing costs; selling expenses; the customers' costs? Second, the choice of full, partial (e.g. direct cost) or variable cost must be made. Third, a decision will be made on how tight the target cost is to be set, for example:

(1) theoretical level of target cost (assuming highest standards of efficiency and therefore the most difficult to achieve);
(2) expected level [assuming a better than average performance but not reaching the high level of (1)];

(3) average level (assuming industry average standards of performance).

Fourth, the expected production volume, production period, production speed and cost reduction rate must be decided. Fifth, the basis for the target cost must be set, for example the production cost of pilot production, the product cost of first production batch or the product cost during main production runs. The American Department of Defense (1975) set their target cost based on average cost at the mass production stage. Similarly, most Japanese companies set the target cost at the expected cumulative average expected product cost when the manufacturing conditions are relatively stable in the production process. This type of target cost gives managers and designers an incentive to control and reduce costs during the planning, design, manufacturing, preparation and early manufacturing stages of the product's life cycle. If a product has a short total life cycle, it is particularly important to control and reduce costs during the initial stages of the product's life cycle and a target cost can help to achieve this.

The above five points are general management considerations to be taken into account when setting a target cost. However, considerations relating to each specific product must also be recognized when setting a target cost.

Specific product and situational considerations

For a target cost to be set realistically it must be based on the product and situation under consideration. For example, the characteristics of the specific planning and design teams for a particular product must be taken into account. These characteristics would include how experienced the teams are, the numbers in the teams and the planning schedule. The novelty of the product is another important consideration. In addition, the existing and proposed technology at the planning, design and manufacturing stages will be influential. Similarly, the target cost will depend on the type of production system available to the organization. Given the wide range of factors involved, the setting of the target cost must be a participative effort involving representatives from production, engineering, design and marketing.

As illustrated above, different types of target cost exist, e.g. target cost for the planning and design stage, target cost for the product's manufacturing cost, target cost for distribution and target cost for customer costs. However, the basic approach of setting a target cost remains the same. This is illustrated below by describing the setting of a target product cost (Tanaka, 1992).

Three basic methods are used for setting target costs. First, there is the subtraction method which is based on the price of competitors' products. This method works backwards from the market price to derive the target cost. The result may represent a very rigorous target, indeed it may be impossible to achieve using the company's or their subcontractors' existing technology.

The second method for setting target costs is the addition method which is based on the existing technology and past cost data of the company and its subcontractors. Due to its derivation the result is normally quite achievable because it is basically an extension of what has already been happening within the company and its subcontractors. However, the addition method is very inward looking and ignores the market situation. Indeed it is questionable whether it should not be simply termed a standard cost rather than a target cost. The result may be an uncompetitive target. As a result of this a third method for setting target costs has been developed.

The third method is the integrated method, a mixture of the subtraction and addition methods. The target cost results from the two methods are 'integrated' by strong leadership from top management and this 'integrated' target cost becomes a management guideline for the company. In practice this integrated method involves solving many difficult problems and conducting a great deal of negotiation. The mechanics of setting a target cost using each of these methods is described in more detail below.

Subtraction method

The critical factor in establishing the target product cost by the subtraction method is the price charged by competing companies:

target cost = selling price − required profit.

The type of target cost varies with the type of expected profit. For example, if the expected profit is gross profit, the target cost is for the full product cost. However, if the expected profit is only contribution, then the target cost is for only the variable costs of the product. In practice, the target costs reflecting the full product cost are by far the most common.

Full product cost

The target cost for the full product cost can be calculated as follows:

$$\text{target cost} = \text{price} - \left(\text{price} \times \frac{\text{gross profit}}{\text{sales}} \right).$$

The price will be determined after considering the expected future state of that particular market and the expected competition. It therefore represents an estimate which requires a great deal of market information and also much expert judgement as, especially where the product is new, the price is expected to be highly variable or price differentiation is expected to exist. However, this is the way in which future expectations about the market are formally incorporated into the management accounting information system. The gross profit/sales ratio (i.e. the gross profit percentage) should represent the future expected gross profit of that particular product, usually earned during the stage when the product is at an established level of output.

Two points should be remembered when calculating this type of target cost. First, in the above formula the future expected gross profit of that product is linked to the gross profit for that product group and also to the corporate level of future expected gross profit. It should fit the financial plans of the organization. Second, although this target cost has been established initially from a market perspective, in practice it will be evaluated and subject to some modification by the internal cost estimating system. It is important, therefore, that this market-based target cost and the internally estimated cost should be expressed in comparable terms. However, in practice there are many examples where these have differed.

Although the full product target cost is common, it includes costs which planners and designers cannot control, e.g. idle capacity costs and many general factory management costs. For cost management purposes, therefore, sometimes the target cost is set to include only the controllable costs related to a particular product.

Addition method

When the addition method is used to help establish the target cost, the focus is on internal factors and capabilities. These include the level of technology, the production plant and machinery, the date of delivery, the production volume and the business strategy. Three ways of using the addition method to set a target cost can be used.

Based on similar products

In this case the target cost is based on similar products or, if segmented, on similar blocks of components. This means that its achievement is usually possible by repeating or, more usually, by at least marginally improving on past performance. Such a target cost can be derived from historical databases on cost reflecting past production experience. In Japan these are known as cost tables (see Chapter 7).

There are three critical steps in setting a target cost in this way. First, the actual cost of similar products must be adjusted to exclude abnormal costs and take into account factors such as the volume of production and inflation rate. These require some assessment of future economic and market conditions and although the emphasis is internal this method of setting target cost does involve some consideration of the external environment.

Second, the target cost is based on the adjusted normal actual costs of groups or lines of products. Figure 4.3 illustrates how 'similar products' or groups of products are chosen. Setting a target cost based on similar products is relatively easy but less accurate. Third, the target cost is set to motivate improvements on past performance.

Based on design properties

Setting a target cost based on the most important design properties of a product (such as the cubic capacity of an engine or the length of a conveyor belt) involves statistical techniques such as regression analysis and factor analysis. The simplest approach is to use past data on similar products to find the relationship between one specific key property of the design and normal actual cost. This can be based on a simple regression equation such as:

$$\text{target cost} = a + bx,$$

where a and b are constants and x is the most important property of design. One relationship which has proved to be very useful in practice is:

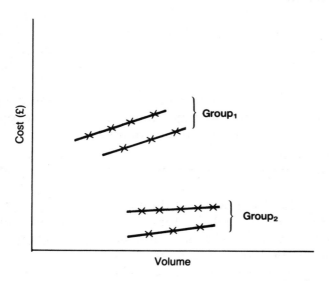

Figure 4.3 Choosing similar products.

$$\text{target cost } a \left(\frac{x_1}{x_2} \right)^n$$

where a is a constant x_1 is the most important old property of the design and x_2 is a new property of the design. (In practice it has been found that n is approximately 0.6~0.7).

These basic statistical approaches can be developed further by applying multiple regression and/or factor analysis to data on multiple properties of a product design and normal actual cost. A final 'rule of thumb' often adopted is based on the number of extra product functions (see Chapter 5) for examples

$$\text{Target cost} = \text{cost of main functions}$$
$$\times \left(1 + \frac{\text{number of extra functions}}{\text{number of existing functions}} \right).$$

Based on new idea

This method of setting the target cost is used when some basic functions or some key aspects of the design of the product are based on a new idea not previously used by the organization. In this case, if the new idea is feasible and gives good cost reduction opportunities, the Japanese experience is that the target cost of the new product and function can be set initially at about 50% of the normal cost of the product which is to be replaced (Tsuchiya, 1967). Again, this provides a basic 'rule of thumb' for setting the target. New ideas underlying this approach would include major new design for the product, new components and new production methods.

Where the basic idea for the new product design is quite similar to that for existing products, experience suggests that the new target cost will be about 70% of the current product cost (Tsuchiya, 1967). Rules of thumb based on the experience of practitioners are helpful for cost management purposes because they give quick initial 'ball-park' figures against which the detailed build-up of a target cost can be assessed. For example, if the detailed target cost can be assessed. For example, if the detailed target cost for a product is calculated at 90% of the cost of the existing product, the rules of thumb would suggest close analysis of the reasons for such target costs. Very often good reasons may exist for such target costs but, from the cost management viewpoint, it is important to understand the special reasons which cause them to vary from the norms.

Integrated method

The above addition method of setting a target cost has clear similarities with the method of setting a standard cost as it tends to ignore one critical feature of the target cost management process, which is to take account of the market situation. However, the addition method has an important role to play in the integrated method. The integrated method combines this addition method (which is based on existing technology and capabilities) and the subtraction method (which is based on the market approach). It can be particularly helpful in increasing the motivation of the designers who may find it difficult to identify with the subtraction method on its own.

The integrated method involves a process of negotiation once the results of the subtraction and addition methods are available. The basic idea is that the integrated target cost should provide a reconciliation of the two methods and give a resultant target which is set from a long-term point of view. Each person in the team involved in the negotiations comes from a different functional background. This stimulates discussion and ideas, although it does make it more difficult to reach a consensus. In the few cases where it is impossible to reach a consensus, top management will make the final decision on the target cost. However, such cases are to some extent failures because an important element of the target cost process is for everyone to identify personally with the final target cost. The target cost has an important motivational element and if the designers, for example, do not accept it then their efforts to achieve it may well be adversely affected. Frequently, the behavioural difficulties in cost management can be at least as important as the technical problems.

ASSIGNMENT OF TARGET COST

The above discussion of target cost setting implies that the target cost is set at a very general level, e.g. as a total figure for a product. This is normally the case at the stage of establishing the target. When efforts begin to achieve the target, however, it is usually necessary to subdivide it and assign it to functions of the product, blocks of components and even to individual cost items. The major function of a pen is 'to make a mark' but subsidiary functions are also required, such as a utility function 'to add colour' and a protective function 'to prevent stains'. A greater explanation of functions, function areas and functional analysis is given later in Chapter 5.

If the target cost is assigned to the lowest possible level, it is easier at a later stage to compare the target costs with the actual costs and, if necessary, to analyse the reasons for a particular target cost not being achieved. The work breakdown structure is one method of assigning the target cost and others include the assignment of target cost to one or more of the following:

(1) the functions or function areas of a product;
(2) blocks of components;
(3) cost items;
(4) activities (such as purchasing or maintenance);
(5) individual designers or a team of designers.

Experience has shown that generally the earlier the target cost is assigned during the planning and design stage for a new product, the better the end result. Assigning the target cost to blocks of components restricts the designers and often leads to the new product being quite similar to existing products. In contrast, by assigning the target cost to the functions of a product, the designers have more freedom in terms of achieving the target cost using alternative design approaches. The basic idea behind the assignment of the target cost is to provide a guideline rather than a straitjacket for designers and, for this reason, the latter approach is generally preferable.

A recent survey of Japanese companies by Yoshikawa (1992) revealed a range of methods of assigning the target cost. There

Table 4.1 Assignment of target cost

	No. of reporting companies	Reporting companies (%)
Target costs are not assigned	9	11
Target costs are assigned:		
(a) to individual functions of the products	8	10
(b) to groups of functions of the products	24	29
(c) to groups of components	15	18
(d) to groups of functions and then to individual functions of the products	13	15
(e) in other ways	4	4
No response	11	13
	84	100

were 84 responding companies across a wide range of industries and the results to the question 'How would your total product target cost be segmented in order to make it more meaningful to the design team?' are shown in Table 4.1. This survey revealed that by far the most common method used by Japanese companies to assign their target costs for products is to the functions of the products (44% of the reporting companies). In contrast, only 18% of the responding companies assigned their target costs to blocks of components of the product.

One potential problem is assigning target cost to major functions is that progress towards the achievement of the target cost must be monitored. This means that a relationship must exist between the target cost assignment and the cost information available to the teams so that actual expected costs can be reported in comparison with each function's target cost.

The method of assigning target cost to functions or function areas, blocks of components and individual cost items will now be considered in more detail.

ASSIGNMENT TO FUNCTIONS

A product has certain functions which combine to achieve its main purpose. Such functions can be grouped into function areas and the target cost can be assigned to these function areas. The underlying reason for assigning the target cost to function areas is to allow the designers as much freedom as possible in using their creative talents to design new or revised products within the target cost guideline.

Three steps are involved in assigning the target cost to function areas. First, the function areas must be defined. Second, the importance of each function area must be evaluated. Third, the target cost must be assigned to each function area based on the relative importance of each function area.

Defining function areas

The definition of the function areas is usually based on the product specification and, from these defined functions, a functional family tree can be drawn. Figure 4.4 shows the broad outline of a functional family tree. A more detailed example of a functional family tree can be found in Figure 5.1. From the functional family tree, the functions can be grouped together into function areas depending on the relationships between the functions and also on the level of the functions, namely upper level, middle level and lower level functions (Figure 4.4). For example, function area 1 includes upper level function FA_1, middle level functions FA_{11} and FA_{12} and lower level functions F_{11-1}, F_{12-1} and F_{12-2}. A similar analysis can be applied to function areas 2 and 3. This shows how the designers can be given some flexibility in terms of how they meet the target cost as they work by broad function area rather than being restricted to trying to achieve the target cost for each specific lower level function.

Evaluating function areas

When evaluating function areas, the decision must be taken whether the evaluation is from the customer's or the manufacturer's viewpoint. The customer perspective is the one which best suits the initial evaluation because the essence of target cost management is to take account of the market requirements.

There are two methods of evaluating function areas, namely by monetary values and by ratios. The monetary approach involves the customers estimating the monetary amount which

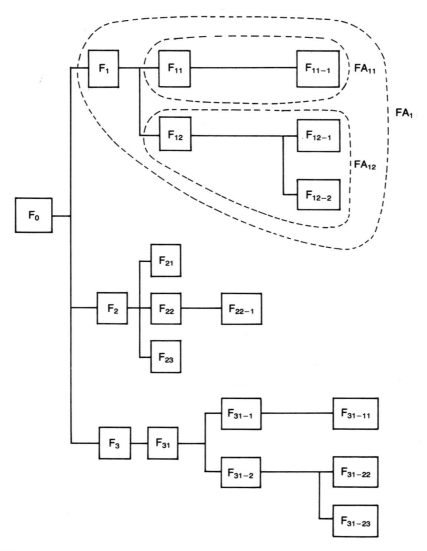

Figure 4.4 Functional family tree and function areas. F, function; FA, function area.

they would be willing to pay for each function or function area. The ratio approach means that customers consider all the functions of a product to represent 100% and then they divide this 100% between the different function areas in a way which reflects the importance of each function area to them. In practice, market research can be used to gather data from customers about their views on different functions and function areas.

Target for functional areas

Although the preferred method of evaluating the function areas is from the consumers' viewpoint using monetary values or ratios, setting such a target cost based solely on the customers' viewpoint may overlook certain factors. These include technical considerations, and meeting safety and other laws and regulations. Although the customers' evaluation should remain dominant, it is often modified in relation to certain function areas to take into account the manufacturer's evaluation before finalizing the target cost for each function area.

Table 4.2 gives an example of how to assign target cost to function areas using the ratio method. The total target cost for the product is £300 000 and the consumers have indicated that functions 1 and 3 are the most important with weightings of

Table 4.2 Assigning target cost to function areas

Function area	Importance of function area from consumers' viewpoint (%)	Amount of target cost assigned (£)
1	27	300 000 × 27% = 81 000
2	20	× 20% = 60 000
3	32	× 32% = 96 000
4	16	× 16% = 48 000
5	5	× 5% = 15 000
	100	300 000

27% and 32%, respectively, giving target costs of £81 000 and £96 000, respectively.

ASSIGNMENT TO COMPONENT BLOCKS

Normally the preferred method of assigning target cost is based on functions. However, in some cases it may be more convenient for planners and designers to assign the target cost of a product to blocks of components. However, as mentioned above, if a target cost is assigned to blocks of components at an early stage in the planning and design process, this generally eliminates new or radical ideas for the design of the product. Assigning target cost to blocks of components is therefore inappropriate for new or complex products. However, where the product is at a relatively late stage in its product life cycle or is relatively simple and where radical improvements to the product are not expected, the method of assigning a target cost to blocks of components may be appropriate. The procedure is as follows:

(1) group the components of the product into various blocks;
(2) evaluate the importance (usually in terms of estimated cost) of each block of components based on the team's experience of similar products;
(3) assign the target cost to each block of components based on this evaluation.

This method can also be combined with the functional approach by assigning the target cost to function areas and then assigning each function area to component blocks. The major difficulty with this combined method is determining the relationships between the function areas and the component blocks. Various combinations are possible:

(1) one function area to one component block;
(2) one function area to several component blocks;
(3) several function areas to one component block;
(4) several function areas to several component blocks.

The first combination poses no problems in assigning the target cost to the component block. However, in the second combination the target cost must be subdivided depending on the number of component blocks. The third combination is an unusual case and is in fact a special case of the fourth combination which usually poses severe problems in assigning the target cost to the component blocks. What generally happens is that a matrix is established relating the function areas to the component blocks (Table 4.3). Here the total target cost of the product for the three function areas is £10 000 and this is assigned to three component blocks as shown by the percentages. The result is that the target cost for component block A is £3600, £2600 for B and £3800 for C.

ASSIGNMENT TO COST ITEMS

The extent to which target cost is subdivided depends mainly on the degree of complexity and novelty of the product design. If it is a completely new product in a technologically complex field, the assignment of target cost will only be at a very general level to function areas. In contrast, if the product is simple and requires only low level technological expertise, it may be appropriate to subdivide the target cost to lower level function areas and to component blocks. Further subdivision of the target cost can be achieved by assigning it to cost items from the component blocks. Cost items can be classified as

Table 4.3 Function areas and component blocks

Function	Target cost of function area (£)	Component block and target cost (£)		
		A	B	C
1	5000	2500 (50%)	1000 (20%)	1500 (30%)
2	3000	900 (30%)	1200 (40%)	900 (30%)
3	2000	200 (10%)	400 (20%)	1400 (70%)
Total	10 000	3600	2600	3800

direct materials, direct labour and overhead costs. Occasionally the latter two are combined as one conversion cost figure. Basically the classification of cost items will be determined by the degree of control required of actual costs at a later stage in the product life cycle. The important point to remember is that the more the target cost is subdivided, the greater are the restrictions placed on the planners and designers and the less likely it is that new ideas will emerge.

ASSIGNMENT TO DESIGNERS

In some organizations target cost is assigned to designers. Normally, it is assigned to a large group of designers, then subdivided to smaller groups of designers and finally to individual designers. The team leader of the large group of designers will decide who is going to plan and design specific function areas or component blocks. This assignment of target cost to small groups of designers, or even to individual designers, will help the team leader to monitor and control the progress of the design team. It is a type of responsibility accounting with the main objective of making the designers cost conscious and motivated to ensure that the overall target cost for the new or revised product is achieved.

CONCLUSION

Target cost management is fundamental to effective cost management because it provides the goal towards which all cost control efforts are directed. It differs from conventional cost management practice through its derivation, at least in part, from the market. In this way, it ensures that the management accounting system is generating information which will help the organization to maintain and enhance its competitiveness. It also encourages innovation and creativeness by focusing in a more abstract way on the product and its cost. The product is no longer taken as given. This is done by analysing and costing its service potential rather than its physical form through using functions and function areas as the basic cost objects of the system. This guides product development towards the generation of cost-effective new products which are innovative and which match customers' technical and price requirements.

REFERENCES

American Department of Defense (1975) Department of Defense Director 5000.28, *Design to Cost*, Department of Defense, Washington.

Carsberg, B. (1975) *The Economics of Business Decisions*, Penguin, New York.

Heyel, C. (1982) *The Encyclopaedia of Management*, 3rd edn, Van Nostrand Reinhold, Amsterdam.

Newbrough, E.T. (1967) *Effective Maintenance Management*, McGraw-Hill, New York.

Tanaka, M. (1988) *Cost engineering system at design phase of new products*. Pacific Basin Value Engineering Conference, proceedings. pp. 192–198.

Tanaka, M. (1992) *Cost and profit engineering system in the product design stage in Japanese companies*. International Federation of Scholarly Associations of Management (IFSAM) conference, proceedings pp. 144–147.

Tanaka, M. Amagasa, M. and Aman, T. (1985) *Determination of manufacturing cost target by design parameter in development of new products*. International Conference on Product Innovation Management (ICPIM), proceedings pp. 227–237.

Tsuchiya, H. (1967) *Significance and methods of the evaluation of function*. Society of American Value Engineers (SAVE), proceedings.

Yoshikawa, T. (1992) Comparative study of cost management in Japan and UK. *Yokohama Business Review*, **13**, June.

CHAPTER FIVE

Functional analysis

INTRODUCTION

Functional analysis is a cost management technique which has developed for value engineering. Value engineering can be defined as:

A systematic interdisciplinary examination of factors affecting the cost of a product or service in order to devise means of achieving the specified purpose most economically at the required standard of quality and reliability. (British Standard 3138)

Among the factors 'affecting the cost' of the product are functions which are built into it and these are central to value engineering. Functional analysis is based on this aspect of value engineering. It is a group activity using the functions of a product or service as the basis for cost management. In Western cost accounting the full product or its physical parts are the most common cost objects. In contrast, functional analysis uses the functions of the product as the cost objects. For example, the major function of a staple remover is 'to take off staples' or the major function of a pen is 'to make a mark'. The function provides an abstract (not tangible or physical) repre-

This chapter is a revision of an earlier paper published in the *Journal of Cost Management*, Spring, 1989, pp. 14–19. Original material and artwork are reprinted with kind permission of the publisher, Warren, Gorham & Lamont.

sentation of the product in terms of the service potential which it offers the customer. In this respect it contrasts markedly with conventional cost accounting. At present, functional analysis is most commonly applied during the development of new products or in the redesign of existing products but it is now also occasionally being applied in other areas, such as services, overheads, organization structure and even to the overall strategy of a company.

The basics of functional analysis were developed in the West (Creasy, 1973) and used by Western companies such as Univac–Sperry Rand, Ford Tractors, General Electric and Chrysler. It has now been widely adopted in Japan and today is one of the major cost management techniques in that country (Yoshikawa, 1990). However, it is a technique which has received little attention from accountants, particularly in the West.

Functional analysis is concerned with profit improvement which may include both cost reduction and also the process of improving products by adding new features in a cost-effective way. Employees from a number of different departments (such as accounting, production, purchasing, engineering, design and marketing) will be involved in the functional analysis team. Well-defined objectives are set for the work of these teams. For example, the objectives may be to reduce the weight of the product by 30% and to reduce the cost of the product by 20% while maintaining the existing quality level of the product. It should be remembered that functional analysis can be applied throughout all the stages of a product's life cycle. However, it is a powerful tool if used at the initial planning and design stages of a new product where costs have still to be committed. There are two types of functional analysis: for the 'first look value engineering (VE)' and the 'second look VE'. The basic procedures for both are similar. Functional analysis for the first look VE is used when developing a new product and is discussed at the end of this chapter. However, most of this chapter will concentrate on functional analysis for the second look VE which is used when changing the design of existing products.

BASIC STEPS

The technique of functional analysis mainly involves the following nine basic VE steps with functional analysis concentrating on (3) to (6) but also including all nine steps:

(1) choose the object of analysis, such as product, service or overhead area;
(2) select members of a team;
(3) gather information;
(4) define the functions of the object;
(5) draw a functional family tree;
(6) evaluate the functions;
(7) suggest alternatives and compare these with the target cost;
(8) choose the alternatives for manufacturing;
(9) review the actual results.

The first step of selecting the object of analysis is critical to the success of the whole activity. If we assume that this functional analysis activity is going to examine existing products (i.e. functional analysis for second look VE), what criteria can be used to choose a particular product as the subject? Suitability is indicated by characteristics such as the total cost involved, the complexity of the product and the bulkiness or weight of the product. Therefore, a heavy, high volume product with a complex design and relatively large production costs is often an ideal candidate for the functional analysis activity.

Once the product has been chosen the second step is to organize the team. Usually it will consist of six to eight members with different skills. This mix of skills and the interaction of team members is critical to the success of functional analysis. To ensure appropriate experience and knowledge, the team members are usually seconded temporarily from their normal job in the company.

The third step of gathering information about the product will include information from both inside and outside the organization. Internal information will include specification or product requirement, detailed design, manufacturing, marketing and cost information. External information will include both internal cost information and also information from outside the company, e.g. on new technologies. This information can be conveniently provided in the form of cost tables. Sato (1965) defined a cost table as 'a measurement to decide cost and to be able to evaluate the cost of not only existing products but also future products at the very beginning of the design process'. Chapter 7 provides more details about cost tables.

Defining the functional family tree is the basis of the fourth step and this involves defining the functions of the chosen product. Figure 5.1 shows the functional family tree for a propelling ball-point pen. It is a means–end structure (from right to left) composed of all the functions of the product. Each function is defined in terms of a verb and a noun. The major function of a propelling ball-point pen can be described as 'make a mark', but supporting functions are also required, such as 'put colour', 'guide tip' and 'prevent loss'. These, in turn, may also require their own supporting functions.

The fifth step involves formally drawing a diagram of the various functions of the product in the format illustrated in Figure 5.1. This functional family tree uses the function definitions and involves arranging them in a logical order so that a meaningful functional family tree can be drawn. This design should be supplemented by the type of information shown in Table 5.1, which illustrates the relationship between the functions and the parts of the propelling ball-point pen and includes the relevant existing costs.

The sixth step of evaluating the relative value of the functions involves external market information as well as internal cost

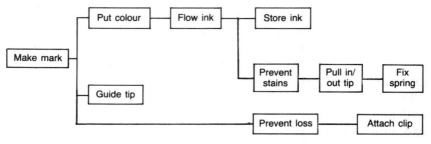

Figure 5.1 Propelling ball-point pen functional family tree.

Table 5.1 Parts, functions and costs

		Function		Cost ($)
Part no.	Name of part	Transitive verb	Noun	
1	Tip	Flow	Ink	0.80
2	Barrel	Guide	Tip	1.20
3	Cartridge	Store	Ink	0.30
4	Top	Store	Ink	0.20
5	Ink	Put	Colour	0.15
6	Cap	Pull in/out	Tip	0.12
7	Spring	Pull in/out	Spring	0.10
8	Stopper	Fix	Spring	0.08
9	Clip	Prevent	Loss	0.13
10	Screw	Attach	Clip	0.02
				3.10

Note: this is an illustrative example. The costs are notional.

information. In this step the existing cost of each function is compared against the target cost, $2.39 in this case. Therefore, this target cost has to be assigned to each function based on the relative value of each function from the customers' viewpoint. The relative value of each function to the customer can be estimated in two main ways. The best method is to ask the customers what they would be willing to pay for each individual function of the product, such as 'prevent loss'. Basically this is a type of market research and it can be quite costly and time- consuming but usually the benefits outweigh the costs. A cheaper, faster, but less accurate method of estimating the relative value of each function to the customer is for each member of the functional analysis team to act as a customer and to place a value on each function. For each function the different values selected by all the team members are discussed and after this discussion a consensus is reached on the relative value and the monetary value for each function. Table 5.2 gives the existing costs for the propelling ball-point pen example and the total target cost of $2.39 assigned in terms of the relative value of each function to the customer. Therefore, this value to the customer in effect gives a target cost for each function (see Chapter 4).

Table 5.2 Costs and values of functions

Functions	(a) Actual cost ($)	(b) Relative value to the customer (%)	(c) = $2.39 × (b) Assignment of target cost based on customers relative function value ($)*	$(d) = \dfrac{(c)}{(a)}$ Value ratio
Flow ink	0.80	25	0.60	0.75
Guide tip	1.20	50	1.20	1.00
Store ink	0.50	12	0.29	0.58
Put colour	0.15	6	0.14	0.93
Pull in/out tip	0.22	1	0.02	0.09
Fix spring	0.08	1	0.02	0.25
Prevent loss	0.13	4	0.10	0.77
Attach clip	0.02	1	0.02	1.00
	3.10	100	2.39	

* These figures are rounded.

Table 5.2 shows that in monetary terms the largest excesses of the actual cost over the assigned target cost are for the functions: flow ink, store ink and pull in/out tip. Another way of analysing the data in Table 5.2 is to calculate a value ratio for each function. This can be defined as:

$$\text{value ratio} = \frac{\text{monetary value to the customer as reflected in assigned target cost}}{\text{actual cost}}.$$

If the value ratio is less than 1.0 it is a cause for concern because the actual cost is higher than the target cost or monetary value to the customer. The value ratios in Table 5.2 of 0.09 and 0.25 for pull in/out tip and fix spring, respectively, highlight the problems associated with these two functions. The basic guideline is to examine those functions where the actual cost is greater than the assigned target cost and within such functions to concentrate on those with the highest costs.

Having integrated the market information into the cost management process during this sixth step, the seventh step is critical, it basically involves a brain-storming session where no suggested alternative is rejected without serious consideration. Often what at first sight may seem a highly inappropriate alternative will turn out to be the basis for the final solution. It is during this stage that the team effect can be particularly important, with the various background experience of the team members leading to different approaches which can be explained, discussed and developed. In practice, the alternatives vary widely, for example the use of new materials or parts, a different method of manufacturing the product, suggestions for completely new products or new product functions, modifications to the functions of the product, the combination of different functions or even elimination of certain functions of the product.

Having generated a number of alternatives, the team members must then take the eighth step of assessing them and making the final choice of which to implement. An example of the result of this step is given in Figure 5.2, which shows the revised functional family tree for, in effect, a new less costly product: a disposable ball-point pen developed from the propelling ball-point pen. This shows that the two functions of preventing stains and preventing loss have been combined while the functions of pull in/out and fix spring have been eliminated. The number of parts for the new disposable pen have fallen from ten (Table 5.1) to six (Table 5.3). This has reduced the cost from $3.10 to only $2 and achieved the target cost of $2.39. In effect, a new lower cost product has been developed. However, it would be wrong to give the impression that functional analysis is all about cost reduction. The objective of functional analysis is profit improvement and this can

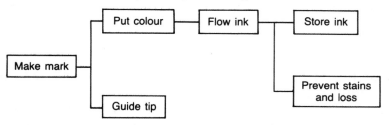

Figure 5.2 Disposable ball-point pen functional family tree.

Table 5.3 Parts, functions and costs

Part no.	Name of part	Function		Cost ($)
		Transitive verb	*Noun*	
1	Tip	Flow	Ink	0.50
2	Barrel	Guide	Tip	1.00
3	Cartridge	Store	Ink	0.20
4	Top	Store	Ink	0.10
5	Ink	Put	Colour	0.12
6	Cap	Prevent	Stain Loss	0.08
				2.00

involve modifications to functions or the addition of new functions in order to improve the worth (and also the price) of the product to the customer.

To ensure that the potential results of the functional analysis are realistically assessed and are not over-optimistic, the ninth step is to promptly conduct an audit or review of the changes implemented. The auditor will report his findings to top management. The reasons for this audit or review are not only to prevent over-optimistic assessments of the functional analysis exercise but also to provide feedback so that future functional analysis can be improved.

WORKSHEETS

To run functional analysis for the second look VE, worksheets are available which can help both to structure and to document the functional analysis process. They provide a step by step guide to the process of functional analysis. Table 5.4 summarizes the series of worksheets needed.

The first worksheet summarizes the characteristics and reasons for the selection of the product for the functional analysis activity. The description of the product will include a rough diagram on this first worksheet. The reasons for selecting the particular product could include apparently high cost, low yield rates, manufacturing problems, market demand (such as remodelling required), or requirement for or more compact design.

Table 5.4 Function analysis: worksheet series*

Worksheet	Content
1	Product choice justification
2	Product characteristics and statistics
3	Function definition
4	Functional family tree
5	Function cost analysis
6	Market perceptions
7	Target costs
8	Alternative suggestions
9	Chosen alternatives
10	Cost savings and profit gains
11	Summary of final recommendations
12	Action required

* These are modifications of the worksheets of the Sanno Institute of Management.

The second worksheet summarizes various types of information such as the annual quantity sold, market, manufacturing and cost information. The market information would include how the product is currently used, the competing products and how these differ from the product under analysis (such as design, capacity or size). The manufacturing information would include details about any problems with suppliers, the proportion of subcontracted components, scrap and any weak points in the manufacturing process (such as capacity problems or the technology being out of date). In addition to the basic cost information, a comparison would be made with the cost of competing products on a total cost basis and also on a cost breakdown basis, such as how overheads compare with those of competitors.

The third worksheet defines the functions and is also helpful to distinguish the primary and secondary functions on the functional family tree. It also includes the existing parts associated with each function (i.e. part number, part name and brief sketch if appropriate) and the function itself defined in terms of a verb and a noun. At this stage it is important to note any restrictions on the functions. For example, there may be specific government regulations or particular specifications from the customer or constraints on the final product if a component is being examined, and such restrictions should be noted against that particular function. Each function should also be classified as a basic or secondary function in terms of the importance of that particular function for that product.

The fourth worksheet is the functional family tree for the existing product. Two helpful tips in drawing a functional family tree are given below.

(1) Keep asking 'how?' when moving from the left to right in a functional family tree, i.e. from primary to secondary functions. For example, in Figure 5.1 'how do you make mark' is answered by 'put colour' and 'guide tip'. Similarly, 'how do you put colour' is answered by 'flow ink' and 'store ink'.

(2) Once you have made your first attempt at drawing the functional family tree you can assess it by asking 'why?' when moving back through the functional family tree from right to left. For example, in Figure 5.1 the answer to 'why do you attach clip' is 'to prevent loss'. Similarly, the answer to 'why do you put colour' is 'to make mark'. This questioning can often reveal flaws in the first draft of the functional family tree.

The fifth worksheet allows a cost analysis of each function or group of functions. It is usually possible to group certain functions. For example, in Figure 5.1 the functions could be grouped as follows:

(1) put colour, flow ink and store ink;
(2) prevent stains, pull in/out tip and fix spring;
(3) guide tip;
(4) prevent loss and attach clip.

Obviously, some details are lost by grouping the functions in this way but it may save considerable time where the product is complex. For the existing product, the costing of the functions will involve a costing of the existing parts used to achieve these functions. The costs will be full costs analysed into material, labour and overhead elements. It will generally help the cost management process if the overheads are expressed in activity cost terms related to their cost drivers. (see Chapter 8)

It is in the sixth worksheet that the market element is formally incorporated into the functional evaluation. This worksheet lists the individual functions (or groups of functions) and the 'cost' of each function from the customers' perspective. This is computed by applying the customers' assessment of the relative value of each function to the total target cost (denoted as C_t). However, occasionally this column is completed by using figures obtained on what the customer would be prepared to pay for each function. The figures in this column can be compared with the existing actual cost of each function, which can be called C_a. The ratio C_t/C_a is then calculated for each function to determine potential problem functions where this ratio is less than 1. However, such functions may be low cost functions and therefore another important criterion is the absolute amount of money involved, which is shown by $C_a - C_t$. The primary and secondary functions will again be identified and the problem functions will be listed in terms of priority for action. This priority is determined basically by C_t/C_a and $C_a - C_t$. Any immediate alternatives should also be noted at this stage so that the ideas raised by drawing the functional family tree are not lost.

On worksheet 7 the existing functional family tree is drawn based on the new target costs derived both from the initial objectives set at the beginning of the functional analysis activity and also from the customers' views of the relative value of each function. This functional family tree will also include the C_a for each function, i.e. the existing actual cost of each function.

The creative core of functional analysis is summarized on worksheet 8 which lists all the alternatives for improvements to the various functions. Usually a separate worksheet will be required for each function or group of functions. In addition to summarizing the alternatives in narrative form it is also helpful to include rough sketches whenever possible. The various alternatives are also evaluated in two ways. First, the viability is assessed and, second, its financial feasibility is considered. After all the alternatives have been made, evaluated and discussed, the members will vote on them to establish the priority ranking. They will then discuss this priority ranking to ensure that they all understand it and, if necessary, another vote will be taken to ensure that the final decision is reached by consensus and is sound from a marketing viewpoint.

Having selected the priority suggestions from their list of alternatives, these ideas will be detailed on worksheet 9. Again, usually a separate worksheet is required for each alternative. This will highlight the function or functions involved and detail the suggested change. The advantages and disadvantages of this change will also be summarized. Sometimes the need for even further information on the suggested change will also be noted. Finally, the type of action required will be highlighted. For example, this alternative may change the design of the product or it may mean using a different supplier for a new material.

The estimated costs and cost savings or profit improvement are summarized on worksheet 10. This gives the name and number of the alternative for the product and the annual sales of that product. The particular function or functions involved are also detailed together with a rough sketch of the existing situation and the proposed alternative. Costs are then calculated both for the existing function and the new proposed function. These costs include the direct material, labour and other costs to give a direct cost per unit. The **incremental** overhead costs for the new alternative are also estimated. It is at this stage that the existence of an activity-based costing system (see Chapters 8 and 9) can assist in linking overhead costs to the proposed functions. The net saving from this new suggestion can be estimated as follows:

(1) saving of direct cost per unit;
(2) total units;

(3) total saving of direct cost (1×2);
(4) incremental overhead;
(5) total net cost saving $= 3 - 4$.

(Note: where the product life is long, discounting may be done to produce a net present value of the savings.)

This worksheet will include any unanswered questions and also a reference to where more information can be found about this proposal.

Worksheet 11 is a summary list of all the recommendations resulting from the functional analysis. It summarizes the profit improvement from all the proposals but also adjusts for any interconnected profit improvements from the various proposals. In other words, the total profit improvement may be less than the total profit improvement from all the individual proposals because of overlap between the improvements to different functions.

The final worksheet summarizes the action required following the functional analysis. It divides the action required into immediate, short-term and long-term action, with a deadline date and the name of the person responsible against each particular action. However, these worksheets are provided as guidelines and should be amended according to the requirements of the specific situation for each functional analysis. Their use is particularly beneficial in giving a logical structure to the functional analysis effort and in providing a clear record of what has been done and achieved.

IMPLICATIONS OF FUNCTIONAL ANALYSIS FOR MANAGEMENT ACCOUNTANTS

If functional analysis is used extensively by a company, a logical development for the costing system is to incorporate costs by functions as well as by parts. If this is done it assists the management accountant in making a timely and active contribution to the whole process. However, rather than simply categorize costs in their conventional classifications of material, labour and overhead it will be valuable if the system is set up to identify the avoidable costs associated with each function. A function's avoidable costs may include both costs which vary with the level of output (such as material costs) and also conventionally classified 'fixed costs', which although unaffected by product volume changes are in fact avoidable if a function is eliminated. For example, one function may require a particular machine and if that function is eliminated, fixed costs such as the machine insurance and maintenance would be avoided.

To measure the real worth of cost savings to the organization the accountant must explore the impact of changes on future cash flows and ideally translate these into a net present value through discounting them at the cost of capital. Conventional cost information provides only a starting point for gathering this information. As Table 5.5 shows, consideration must be

Table 5.5 Cash flow implications of functional analysis

	Cost of function being eliminated (per unit) (£)	Cash flow implications
Material and parts	200	(1) Expected future acquisition price of material and parts over the remaining life of the product (2) Savings in storage (3) Proceeds from disposal of stock
Direct labour	100	(1) Expected future wages to be paid from time when employee can contractually be made redundant (2) Redundancy payments
Production overheads	300	(1) Savings in future payments at approximate date from which cessation is possible (2) Exclusion of any depriciation charges Extra taxation to be paid on higher profits from the change

given to factors such as the timing of the commencement of the cash saving, the disposal process of resources no longer needed, the elimination of costs, such as depreciation which do not involve cash outflows, and the taxation payment implication of the change.

Two techniques which will help management accountants to contribute to the functional analysis process are cost tables and activity-based costing. Both of these cost management techniques are discussed in detail in Chapters 7 and 8, respectively, but briefly cost tables give the management accountant (and others) access to cost information about alterations to the materials, product design and production processes presently being used by the company. This means that the cost tables enable the management accountant to cost the various alternatives proposed by the functional analysis members promptly. Similarly, an activity-based costing system will give the management accountant useful information about what drives specific overheads within the organization. These cost drivers can then be used to link overhead cost to individual functions or groups of functions so that when a function is changed, a basis for ascertaining the effect (if any) on the overheads is readily available.

ADVANTAGES

Perhaps the main advantage of functional analysis is the competitive advantage resulting from improved, cost-effective design or redesign of products. However, functional analysis has also been applied to services, particular overhead areas, the restructuring of organizations and even to corporate strategy. Its ability to view such objects in abstract (service potential) terms rather than physical (parts and people) terms gives functional analysis a flexibility in application which renders its potential enormous. The team approach which underlies it reinforces these benefits.

Another advantage of functional analysis is that information about product functions and about the views of customers are integrated into the formal reporting system. Therefore, although functional analysis may be organized as a series of one-off exercises, a system has to be established to supply the relevant cost information on an on-going basis. Indeed, reporting on a functional basis may correspond more closely with the responsibilities of individual managers and this functional reporting may become the basis for a new system of responsibility accounting in some companies.

Although functional analysis can be applied throughout the product's life cycle, probably the greatest benefits from it can be derived during the planning and design stages for new products. One reason for this is that up to 90% of the costs of many products are in fact committed by the end of the design stage. Functional analysis can play an important role during the planning and design stages because not only does it ensure that multiple skills and experiences are applied to the work but because it can also give useful guidelines to the designers. For example, based on the customers' assessment of a function or group of functions, a target cost can be established for that group of functions, and the specific designers can be set the task of designing the new product with this group of functions within that target cost.

In conclusion, the objective of functional analysis must be kept in mind. It is not simply cost reduction but profit improvement. It is important to remember that a critical aspect of functional analysis is assessing whether or not new functions can be added to the product which will be so attractive to the customer that, although the cost of the product may be increased, the profit from the product is actually increased. Functional analysis is an important cost management tool with its essential features of the team approach, attention to customers' views and concentration on the functions rather than the parts of a product. Functional analysis is an approach which can be applied throughout the product's life cycle and also to other areas such as services and overheads. Every organization should at least consider whether or not functional analysis is an appropriate cost management tool for it to use.

REFERENCES

Creasy, R. (1973) *Functional Analysis System Technique Manual*, Society of American Value Engineers, Irving.

Sato, R. (1965) *Cost Table*, Sangyou Nouritu Junior College, Japan.

Society of Japanese Value Engineering (1992) *VE Terminology*, Tokyo.

Tanaka, M. (1985) *VE (Kachibunseki)*, Managemento-sha, Japan.

Tanaka, M. (1993) *Evaluation of function and value improvement by rating approach*. International Conference on Society of American Value Engineers (SAVE), proceedings. pp. 69–77.

Tanaka, M. (1985) *VE (Kachibunseki)*, Managemento-sha, Japan.

Tanaka, M. (1985) New approach to the function evaluation system in value engineering. *International Journal of Production Research*, Taylor & Francis, Vol. 37, No. 4 pp. 625–637.

Yoshikawa, T. (1990) Comparative study of cost accounting systems in Japan and UK. *Yokohama Business Review*, **10**, March, 58–79.

CHAPTER SIX

Cost estimation

INTRODUCTION

The previous chapters have emphasized the central roles of target cost management and functional analysis in an effective system of cost management. The two are linked through the assignment of target cost to individual product functions. These segmented target costs then represent the key objective for planners and designers. They must find alternatives such as new functional designs, different materials or different manufacturing methods to achieve the target cost. Cost estimation is the means by which they can evaluate whether or not the various alternatives will achieve the target cost. The generation of cost estimates is based on current known conditions, e.g. the present known technology for production. They therefore represent realistically attainable costs. A cost estimation system is necessary to operate target cost management and functional analysis successfully. It provides a control on the designers to permit assessment of the financial viability of their work. This control has to be based on cost estimates because it occurs at the design stage, before costs are committed and before actual costs are known.

The objectives of cost estimation at the planning and design stage are (1) to increase the cost effectiveness of planning and designing products and (2) to achieve the target cost. The cost estimation consists of two functions. First, evaluate the technology plans involved in planning and designing products in cost terms (i.e. current prices based on past experiences, knowledge, and useful information about future costs.) The second function is to predict fluctuations in costs over time.

Thus, the cost estimation has two functions, namely cost evaluation and cost prediction. However, cost evaluation is regarded as cost estimation in a more narrowly defined sense. The main purpose of cost evaluation is to calculate the specification costs of the product. These specification costs are the cost object for cost evaluation presented in this book.

CLASSIFICATION OF COST ESTIMATION

Method

There are two main methods of cost estimation, namely the bottom–up and the top–down approaches. The bottom–up method involves calculating the cost of parts and components and aggregating these costs to calculate the cost of the product. In other words, the bottom–up method is the same as the traditional cost estimation system with the underlying assumption that the product specification and design have already been decided and are fixed.

The limitation of this traditional bottom–up method is that when it is applied at the planning and design stage for a new product, it will give the same result as cost estimation at the manufacturing stage. This means that if the estimation cost is higher than the target cost, the product must be redesigned from scratch and this can be extremely costly, particularly where product life cycles are short. The bottom–up method of cost estimation is therefore less appropriate at the planning and design stage but can be useful during the preparation for manufacturing and in the manufacturing stages of a product's life cycle.

The alternative top–down method of cost estimation is based on the cost data and characteristics of similar functions for products already in existence. This method can be applied during each step of the planning and design process to make realistically approximate cost estimations. The major advantage of the top–down method is that the cost estimating can be done extremely quickly. Its major disadvantage is its requirement for a large volume of cost data about similar functions and function areas.

Cost object

There are two basic cost objects for cost estimation, namely the physical (such as products, components and parts) and the abstract (the service potential offered as evidenced by the functions of a product). As expected, the bottom–up method of cost estimation is associated with the physical product and the top–down method is generally used to estimate the costs of product functions. However, experience has shown that if the product functions are defined carefully, relatively accurate cost estimation figures can be obtained not only for the design stage but also for the later stages in a product's life cycle.

Type of costs

Cost estimation can also be classified on the basis of the type of costs involved. It can include all cost elements or be restricted to partial costs (e.g. prime or direct cost) or incremental costs. Generally, however, estimation is based on full cost, but it is important to be able to switch from full to incremental cost when the situation requires it and also for full cost estimation to be detailed enough to be able to estimate partial cost when necessary.

Level of detail

The cost estimation method used can be either detailed or approximate. The traditional method of cost estimation is the detailed approach which involves aggregating individual costs to calculate a total. Detailed cost estimation is usually combined with the bottom–up approach after the product specification has been fixed. The disadvantages of detailed cost estimation are that it is time-consuming and costly. The approximate method of cost estimation is usually combined with the top–down approach and applied to product functions at the design stage. As its name suggests, the approximate method is less accurate than the detailed method but is much quicker, cheaper and more convenient.

COST ITEMS

Depending on the method of cost estimation used at the planning, design and manufacturing stages, and the desired accuracy of cost estimation, a decision must be made about the detail of the product cost items. For example, the cost items can vary as follows:

(1) total product cost without any subdivisions;
(2) product cost analysed into direct material cost and other cost;
(3) product cost analysed into direct material cost, direct conversion cost and other cost.

The total product cost without any subdivisions may be used for very approximate cost estimation at the very early planning stage. The product cost analysed into direct material cost and other cost gives more accurate cost estimation, but again is used for approximate cost estimation at the early design stage. In contrast, the product cost analysed into direct material cost, direct conversion cost and other cost is the most accurate of the three classifications and is used for detailed cost estimation during the later design stage.

Sato (1986), however, has suggested that instead of the above three-item classification of cost components, it would be more accurate for cost estimation purposes to use a four-item classification as illustrated in Table 6.1. The main reason for the additional category of equipment cost is that with the increase

Table 6.1 Cost components

Traditional classification		New classification
1. Material cost	Raw material and purchased parts Movement and storage	1. Material cost
2. Other cost	Depreciation, insurance, maintenance, electricity and tools	2. Equipment cost
	Travel, transport and consumable supplies	3. Other cost
3. Labour cost	Wages, bonuses, overtime and welfare	4. Labour cost
	Operation of labour office and welfare services	

in automation and robotics, equipment costs have been increasing both in total and also as a percentage of total product costs. For cost management purposes, therefore, it is important that managers plan and control equipment costs during the planning and design stage for a new product. With Sato's classification, the product cost can be defined as:

direct material cost
+ direct conversion cost $\begin{cases} \text{(a) direct labour cost} \\ \text{(b) 'direct' equipment cost} \end{cases}$
+ direct expenses
+ indirect conversion cost
+ factory management cost.

Each of these five product cost components will be considered briefly in the context of cost estimation.

Direct material cost

Direct material cost which comprises the materials, parts and components included in the product can be measured without too much difficulty. However, the direct material cost for cost estimation may also include material-related costs (both internal and external to the company), such as the movement and storage costs of the material and also the material and material-related costs of the subcontractor. This wider approach of including material and material-related costs in the direct material cost enables a more realistic estimate of the full cost implications of parts which designers wish to include in the new product.

Direct conversion cost

Direct conversion cost includes direct labour cost and direct equipment cost.

Direct labour cost

As usual, direct labour cost includes the cost of employees working directly on the product, e.g. on the production line. The cost of such employees includes not only their wages or salaries but also bonuses, pension payments by the company and welfare benefits provided by the company. In addition, the costs of operating the personnel and welfare departments will also be included in the direct labour cost. Again this would be very unusual at present for Western companies. One of the reasons for this wider definition of direct labour cost for cost estimation is to enable comparisons to be made with the cost of using a subcontractor.

Direct equipment cost

Direct equipment cost is the cost of the machines which are used directly in manufacturing the product. The equipment costs will include depreciation, maintenance and other costs directly associated with these machines.

Direct expenses

Direct expenses would include other costs directly associated with the product such as design cost, development cost, subcontractors' conversion cost and cost of moulds, tools and patents.

Indirect conversion cost

Indirect conversion cost includes costs not directly associated with the product such as indirect material cost, indirect labour cost, indirect equipment cost and indirect other cost.

Factory management cost

Factory management cost includes the factory administration and accounting.

TIMING OF COST ESTIMATION

As costs for a new product are frequently subject to substantial learning effect variations it is normal for cost estimation to be undertaken in relation to production costs once the production process is stabilized. Nevertheless, this discussion of the timing of cost estimation should not hide the fact that costs must be controlled throughout the manufacturing stage of the product's life cycle. It is also important to control costs during the first production run as well as during production runs when the product is mature. Indeed, the trend in many industries to much shorter product life cycles has increased the importance of cost management during the first production run. The practical implication of this is that cost estimates for control purposes for both the early and mature stages of production may need to be made.

PROBLEMS OF COST ESTIMATION

The critical importance of estimating costs at the planning and design stage has been emphasized. However, applying the traditional methods of estimating costs at these stages can raise a number of problems. These problems are identified below so that an appreciation is gained of the need for cost estimation.

One problem already mentioned is that traditionally costs are estimated after the product specification and production volumes are decided. This means that if the estimated cost will not achieve the target cost, it is very often too late to make any necessary design changes. Another problem is the detail of cost estimation which requires a great deal of time and also the skills of specialist estimators. Attempts at economizing by doing such cost estimations quickly, usually means a very inaccurate cost estimate. To avoid this, costs should be estimated at as early a stage in the product's life cycle as possible. The results of a survey of Japanese companies in Table 6.2 suggest that earlier cost estimation is the future trend in Japan.

Table 6.2 Timing of cost estimations by Japanese companies

	Current practice (%)	Future intentions (%)
Planning	13	31.3
Basic design	18	26.0
Detailed design	33	20.8
Preparation	27	12.5
No response	9	9.4
	100.0	100.0

Source: response from 97 Japanese companies in a survey by Yoshikawa (1992).

A further problem lies in applying cost estimation only to one product specification. This may often be done in detail on the basis of a bottom–up approach. However, very often such accuracy and attention to detail means that flexibility is sacrificed as no attention has been given to evaluating design alternatives. Generally, it will be more important to evaluate approximately several design alternatives than to evaluate accurately only one design approach.

Finally, the traditional approach to cost estimation assumes an average capacity level but when subcontractors are being considered this may imply capacity changes for the organization. It is then necessary to use different capacity levels in the various cost estimates. In traditional costing these complexities are usually handled by specialist estimators. This gives rise to a major weakness in the traditional approach, i.e. that designers do not evaluate the cost implications of their own designs. In short, the problems of traditional cost estimation can be summarized as follows:

(1) costs are estimated only after product specification has been established;
(2) it is difficult to estimate costs at the early planning stage;
(3) estimates are based on the costs of the physical product rather than the costs of product functions or design properties;
(4) it is difficult and time-consuming to estimate the costs of design changes and design alternatives;
(5) specialist estimators rather than the designers do the cost estimation.

Two approaches which try to minimize the above problems of traditional cost estimation are, first, cost estimation based on the functions of a product and, second, the use of cost tables.

COST ESTIMATION BASED ON FUNCTIONS

Cost estimation has a part to play not only at the detailed design stage but also at the basic design stage. When designers try to evaluate the cost implications of alternative designs at an early stage in the design process, it is almost impossible if the cost estimation system is based on the parts of a product. However, if the cost estimation system is based on the more abstract functions of the product, the designers themselves can make estimates of the costs both relatively accurately and quickly.

At the basic design stage it will usually be necessary to use a large function area and, as expected, the accuracy of the cost estimate will be poorer than the cost estimate at the detailed design stage. A survey found that 65% of designers estimate the costs of their own designs in major Japanese electrical machinery companies, although a substantial minority are still estimating these costs based on the parts rather than on the functions of the product.

COST ESTIMATION BY COST TABLE

Japanese designers and cost estimators will generally use a cost table to help them make their cost estimates (see Chapter 7 for a fuller description of cost tables). Traditional cost tables for estimating purposes were based on the parts of a product but the more recent cost tables for designers are based on the functions of a product. Particularly for designers these cost tables include mathematical formulae showing the relationship between costs and functions. In one recent survey (Yoshikawa, 1992) it was found that almost 17% of Japanese companies linked these cost tables to their computer aided design (CAD) system to make it even easier for designers to see the cost implications of different design alternatives.

For a cost table to provide a realistic basis for estimating costs it is necessary for it to take account of major factors underlying cost variation. This can be done by adjusting the figures gleaned from the cost table.

ADJUSTMENTS BY EXPERIENCE CURVE EFFECT

The learning curve effect became popular in the 1950s with the realization that direct labour hours per unit of product decreased as the workforce climbed the experience curve and learnt how to make the product more quickly. This reduction in direct labour hours led to a decrease in the unit cost of the product. However, cost reduction in a mass-production situation comes not only from the learning curve effect but also from other factors such as the size of the factory, production technology, management method and design modifications. This is known as the experience curve effect.

The experience curve effect can be an important competitive advantage for any company. For example, the unit product cost can be reduced by between 15 and 30% if the cumulative production volume is doubled. The cumulative product cost curve and the average product cost can be calculated based on this experience curve and this can be used to modify the cost estimate from the cost table, or this experience curve can be incorporated into the cost table itself.

ADJUSTMENTS BY SPECIAL FACTORS

Sometimes the cost table may not take into account material losses. For example, material may be lost because of tests or set-ups. The alternatives are to modify the cost estimate, to incorporate such material losses into the cost table or to set-up a special cost table for such material losses.

Another special factor can be the excess time taken depending on the working conditions. One reason for excess time is the group time allowance. For example, if a group work along a conveyor belt, experience has shown that the excess time will vary between 3 and 7% (Tanaka, 1989). Another allowance is the machine allowance which is caused by the delay involved when one person operates multiple machines. This time allowance can be calculated depending on the nature of work, machine interference and number of machines involved. Again some companies now incorporate such special factors in their cost tables to avoid adjustments to cost estimates made from their cost tables.

Particularly in Japan cost tables have become an indispensable part of providing a fast and reliable cost estimation service. Their nature and benefits are explored in Chapter 7.

REFERENCES

Sato, S. (1986) *Clear Cost Accounting*, Chuou-Keizaisha, Japan.

Tanaka, M. (1987) New cost estimating methods at a new product design. *Cost Accounting*, The Japan Cost Accounting Association, No. 22, pp. 58–88.

Tanaka, M. (1989) Cost estimating for a new product design. *SUT Bulletin*, Science University of Tokyo, Japan, **6**, No. 10, pp. 26–32.

Tanaka, M. (1991) Cost estimation system in computer integrated manufacturing (CIM). *Accounting*, The Japan Accounting Association, **139**, No. 2, pp. 202–22.

Yoshikawa, T. (1992) Comparative study of cost management in Japan and UK. *Yokohama Business Review*, **13**, June, 79–106.

CHAPTER SEVEN

Cost tables

INTRODUCTION

One of the major differences between Western and Japanese management accounting is the cost table. Western management accountants have a great deal of costing information on existing products but usually they conduct special one-off exercises to cost new products. Furthermore, Western management accountants in general become involved in the costing of new products after the initial design stage. In contrast, Japanese management accountants and cost estimators have very detailed cost tables or cost databases which provide most of the costing information for new products. Furthermore, with their cost tables Japanese management accountants can quickly provide answers to 'what if?' questions relating to product design alterations. This ability has helped the Japanese management accountant to become an integral part of the design team even at the planning stage for a new product.

DEFINITION

Cost tables have long been used by cost estimators in Japan but it was only in the 1960s that they became known by this

This chapter is a revision of an earlier paper published in the *Journal of Cost Management*, Fall, 1990, pp. 30–6. Original material and artwork are reprinted with kind permission of the publisher, Warren, Gorham & Lamont.

name and received widespread publicity through Ryo Sato's (1965) book *Cost Table*. This book publicized their existence and emphasized to staff other than cost estimators the potential benefits of using cost tables. Sato (1965) defined a cost table as 'a measurement to decide cost and to be able to evaluate the cost of not only existing products but also future products at the very beginning of the design process'.

In contrast to Ryo Sato's definition of cost tables, this book will employ the following, broader definition of cost tables:

A cost table includes data summarized to estimate costs quickly and easily with a certain degree of accuracy for cost estimation purpose such as pricing decisions, decisions for product specification and decisions for production methods and means (Tanaka, 1988).

Cost data tables also contain data essential for cost estimation purposes such as time estimates. The data may be in graphical form, tabular form, and/or an algebraic expression, depending upon the particular application.

Since the mid-1960s the use of cost tables has widened with Japanese managers now using them to help determine product specifications, production methods and best working practices, and also as an input to decisions such as pricing and capital investment appraisal of new machinery.

CLASSIFICATION

Traditionally Japanese cost tables were classified according to the area in which they would be used. Thus tables existed for design, manufacturing, purchasing and distribution (e.g. Tanaka, 1988).

Design

Cost tables play a critical role in the design process and this is reflected in the fact that five different types of cost table are used during various stages in the design process.

Concept design cost table

This cost table is used to evaluate alternative product designs at a very early stage in the conceptual development of a new product. The concept design cost table will be used to evaluate the main potential functions of a new product and it takes a very broad brush approach to allow managers to see the cost implications of different potential designs at the stage when the product is not much more than an idea in the designer's mind.

Basic design cost table

This is a critical cost table because the greatest percentage of product costs are usually determined by decisions made at the basic design stage. Managers can also use the basic design cost table to evaluate the economic performance of the design of various functions of the new and redesigned product. Whenever possible the basic design cost table will try to use charts or mathematical formulae to show the effects of changes in the design and in the functions of the new product.

Design cost table

This is a cost table which designers themselves use to evaluate the specification and economic performance of a new product. Designers use the design cost table particularly to evaluate the economic performance of a new product.

Detailed design cost table

At this stage designers and managers must take many detailed decisions for new products, e.g. type of material, shape, tolerance and surface finish. Such decisions will affect the cost of new products and the detailed design cost table can be used as a basis for quickly estimating their cost impact.

Manufacturing process design cost table

Managers can use this cost table to help them choose between alternative methods of manufacturing product lines. This cost table can also be used as part of the input for the decision regarding which factory should manufacture a new product and also for the decision whether to manufacture a new product at a specific factory within the group or to subcontract the manufacture to another company.

Production cost table

Once the decision has been taken to manufacture a new product in a particular factory, the production cost table can help managers to decide the most beneficial production method assuming a certain band of production volume and related production time requirements.

Purchasing and subcontracting cost table

Probably the most widespread use of cost tables in Japan is in the area of purchasing. Historically, in fact, cost tables were developed for purchasing and particularly for subcontracting decisions. When managers negotiate with subcontractors they can use the purchasing cost table to give up-to-date and accurate estimates of the parts or products to be subcontracted. Indeed there are many examples where subcontractors have gained the contract only after agreeing to install a new type of machine identified by the cost table.

Moulds and tools cost table

A relatively recent development has been the use of moulds and tools cost tables, as the cost of these factors has risen mould and tool cost tables have developed as a sub-set of the purchasing cost table. Given the novelty of this type of cost table a number of Japanese companies still deliberately retain 10% of their mould production in-house specifically so that they can keep their moulds cost table up-to-date and then use it to negotiate prices with subcontractors.

Distribution cost table

Cost tables are not only concerned with the manufacturing process and a good example of this is the distribution cost table. This table gives the cost of alternative means of distributing a product and gives managers a financial basis for choosing between alternative channels of distribution.

In addition to the main method of classifying cost tables by the above areas of use, cost tables can also be classified by the method of estimation and also by the object of cost estimation. The two major methods of estimation are given below.

1. 'Bottom–up' or addition method
   This cost table is used for very detailed estimates and is the most popular method of cost estimation in Japan. This cost table makes it easy to compare the cost of each process stage in the production but it is difficult to keep this cost table up-to-date because of the detail involved.
2. 'Top–down' method
   This cost table is used mainly for rough estimates. It is based mainly on mathematical formulae such as the relationship between the cubic capacity of a motor cycle and its cost. As you would expect, this 'top-down' cost table can be updated relatively easily.

Another important distinction between cost tables is the object of the cost estimation. One type of cost table concentrates on the physical product or blocks of components, i.e. it costs the parts of a product. In contrast an increasingly popular type of cost table concentrates not on the parts but on the individual functions or groups of functions of a product.

BUILDING A COST TABLE

The above classification of cost tables illustrates the range of cost tables. Similarly the assumptions underlying a cost table can vary. For example, four different capacity levels can be used for the cost table:

(1) theoretical capacity level;
(2) practical capacity level;
(3) average capacity level;
(4) expected actual volume.

The theoretical capacity level is the maximum volume attainable in theory ignoring practical constraints. The practical capacity level takes account of practical constraints but it can only be achieved by a great deal of effort. The average capacity level is based on past and current experience and assumes that future experience will be similar to the past. The expected actual volume is based on the plant and machinery capital investment programme, expected changes in technology and the production schedule.

However, probably the most important decision in constructing a cost table is the choice of adoption of the very detailed bottom–up approach or the broad-brush top–down approach. Over the life cycle of a given product these approaches need not be mutually exclusive as it is quite possible to use them at different stages in the product life cycle. For example, a planning cost table will usually adopt a top–down approach whereas a production or purchasing cost table will generally use a bottom–up approach.

BOTTOM–UP APPROACH

With the bottom–up approach there are two distinct methods which have been mentioned already, namely concentrating on either the physical product (or parts of a product) or the functions of a product. The method of constructing a cost table based on the physical product will be described below. The procedures outlined are also those applied to the functions of a product.

The basic rule for the bottom–up approach is that the greater detail in which the cost of a product is to be estimated, the more subdivisions are required of the cost items. To give some indication of the detail involved, the following cost items will be discussed:

(1) direct material cost;
(2) direct conversion cost;
(3) development and design cost;
(4) factory management cost.

Direct material cost table

At the most basic level direct material cost is material price multiplied by volume of material consumption. However, the direct material cost table will include an analysis of the volume of material consumption as in Figure 7.1. The volume of material consumption for manufacturing products will be based initially on existing machines and existing production technology. However, this is very much a starting point only. The volume of material consumption will vary, for example, with material shape, size and accuracy.

The net spending volume of material consumption can be calculated theoretically and statistically from the product specification and detailed plans and to this can be added a volume allowance for the difference between theoretical and practical volume of material consumption. However, in addition to the net volume of material consumption will be added the excess volume of material consumption. This is a minimum margin of safety for material consumption consisting of:

(1) material loss from set-up tests which will include not only practice set-ups but also testing for replacement of tools, tests to estimate defective work and destruction tests;
(2) yield loss which will include defective work and waste;

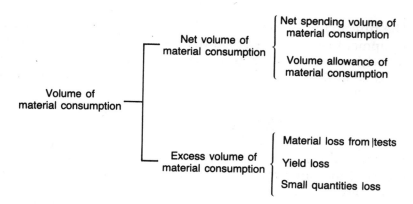

Figure 7.1 Material consumption.

(3) small quantities loss which may arise when the production volume is less than the minimum recommended volume.

The above gives an indication of the detail included in the direct material cost table about the volume of material consumption. Similar details about the price of material will also be included in the cost table.

The cost table will show not only the purchase price of materials but also the following external and internal costs:

(1) external costs such as transport costs, loading costs and insurance;
(2) internal costs such as purchasing department costs, unloading costs, internal inspection and storage costs.

These external and internal costs are traced to specific materials which may involve bases such as number of purchase orders or number of issues of material. The point is that costs which would be overhead costs in the West are classified as material costs in Japanese cost tables. In other words, the Japanese direct material cost table takes a very broad view of materials and includes overhead costs 'caused' by the materials. The underlying objective is to try to charge to the cost object (in this case materials) directly as much as possible and so leave a minimum in the overhead cost.

Direct conversion cost tables

The direct conversion cost table includes direct machine and equipment costs and a broad definition of direct labour costs. As with materials, the basic idea is to include as much as possible in the direct conversion cost. Usually a machine hour rate will be used, such as:

$$\frac{\text{capacity and operating costs of machines}}{\text{expected operating hours}}$$

However, this is too broad and for cost management purposes the machine hour rate will be analysed into various components (Figure 7.2). The two major components are a capacity cost rate including costs such as depreciation, insurance and even lighting, as well as preventative maintenance and an operating cost rate including costs such as electricity, material and tool supplies. The analysis of power costs into direct operating and lighting is to arrive at a more accurate machine hour rate. This machine hour rate can then be multiplied by the number of machine operating hours to calculate a direct machine cost.

The direct labour cost must, of course, be added to this direct machine cost to calculate the direct conversion cost. Basically the labour cost is a labour rate multiplied by the number of working hours. However, again the difference from Western accounting practice is the very broad definition of labour cost which again is mainly for cost management purposes.

The labour cost in the direct conversion cost table includes the wages of direct and indirect employees, the costs of hiring and training employees and even the salary costs of the personnel and payroll departments. This labour cost can then be divided by the annual working hours to calculate the total labour rate.

Development and design cost table

The development and design cost table will include not only the costs of design but also the cost of development, moulds,

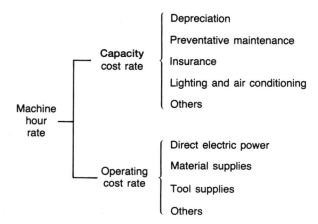

Figure 7.2 Direct machine hour rate.

tools and trial product. This cost table can be based on the new product but usually it is constructed by using a similar product. The disadvantage is a lack of accuracy in the cost table but the advantage is that general relationships can be established between past cost data and various design properties. The cost tables for design and trial products are a relatively new development but they are becoming increasingly important.

Factory management cost table

The direct material, direct conversion cost and development and design cost tables include many costs which Western companies would usually classify as overheads, but the remaining factory overheads would be included in the factory management cost table. Factory management costs are usually included in product cost by means of an overhead rate based on labour hours or operating hours. In other words, budgeted or expected factory management costs are divided by the number of operating hours to give a factory management rate which can then be used in the costing of new products. Depending on the situation a factory wide rate may be used or if this is too inaccurate different overhead rates can be calculated for different parts of the factory, although this tends to be by groups of machines rather than full production department rates. Hopefully, this discussion of four types of cost table gives some indication of the detail available in the bottom–up approach to cost tables. Generally, the bottom–up approach is used in relation to the redesign or modification of existing products. The alternative top–down approach to cost tables can be more easily applied to new products.

TOP–DOWN APPROACH

The top–down approach to cost tables can be based either on the physical product or on the functions of a product.

Based on physical product

When a cost table is based on the physical product, the cost management method of group technology is usually critical. Group technology involves grouping products together on the basis of certain product properties such as size, shape, quality of material, manufacturing method and accuracy. The criteria used to determine the product groups are important, as is the decision about how far to break down the product into its various components. Having established groups of relevant products, the product cost of the group can be shown in a cost table. Experience has shown that such a cost table is quite accurate because it is based on similar products.

Based on function

The cost table which is based on the functions of a product attempts to determine the relationship between the functions (or properties) of the estimation object (usually a product) and its actual cost and this relationship is usually expressed by a chart or mathematical formula. Cost tables based on the functions of a product or service can be classified into those using theoretical values and those using actual values.

Theoretical values

When the relationship between the function of a product and its actual cost can be related to a mathematical formula a cost table can be estimated. Tamai (1981) gives an example of 'transmit torque' which can be expressed for an iron bar as:

$$t = \frac{\pi}{16} s_t d^3, \tag{7.1}$$

where t = torque (kg/cm), s_t is the maximum allowed breaking stress and d is the diameter in centimetres of iron bar.

The cost of an iron bar can be expressed as:

$$c = \frac{\pi}{4} d^2 lgp, \tag{7.2}$$

where c is material cost, d is diameter in centimetres of iron bar, l is length in centimetres of iron bar, g is specific gravity of material (kg/cm^3) and p is material price per kilo.

Equation (7.1) can be expressed as:

$$d = \left(\frac{16t}{\pi\,s_t}\right)^{1/3} \tag{7.3}$$

and equation (7.2) can be expressed as:

$$\frac{c}{l} = \frac{\pi}{4}d^2\,gp. \tag{7.4}$$

From equations (7.3) and (7.4) one can derive:

$$\frac{c}{l} = \frac{\pi}{4}gp\left(\frac{16}{\pi\,s_t}\right)^{2/3}t^{2/3}. \tag{7.5}$$

In equation (7.5)

$$\frac{\pi}{4}gp\left(\frac{16}{\pi\,s_t}\right)^{2/3}$$

is a coefficient which can be fixed by which kind of material is to be used. If we call this coefficient K, equation (7.5) can be expressed as:

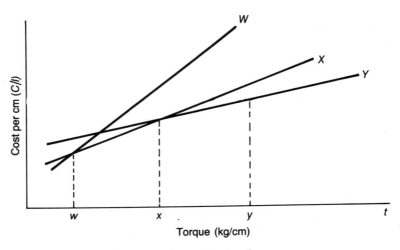

Figure 7.3 Cost and torque theoretical values.

$$\frac{c}{l} = K\,t^{2/3}. \tag{7.6}$$

Using equation (7.6) the costs for different materials can be calculated and this is illustrated in Figure 7.3. To many Western management accountants the above equations and this theoretical approach will seem out of place in a cost management book but this example illustrates that many such cost relationships can be expressed in these terms. What is the usefulness of such a theoretical approach? Figure 7.3 gives the answer. If the size of torque is less than w, then material W's cost is the theoretical cost standard. However, if the size of torque is between w and x, then material X's cost is the theoretical cost standard. Similarly, if the size of torque is between x and y, then material Y's cost is the theoretical cost standard. Many such theoretical relationships are the basis of cost tables.

Actual values

Objective and reliable cost figures can be derived when using theoretical values for establishing a cost table by function. However, this method can be used only when the function level can be measured objectively. A cost table by actual values is a summary of the relationships between function properties and the actual costs of the organization. To produce cost tables by actual values requires groupings of products or components based on function, structure and manufacturing process. Very often regression is used to express the relationships between the actual cost and the functions of a product. This cost table using actual values is growing in importance in Japan although, of course, actual data are required before compiling such a cost table.

The advantage of these cost tables arranged by function can be summarized as follows:

(1) with cost figures for each function, sensitivity analysis can be applied to the costs very easily;
(2) planners and designers can estimate costs easily and, in particular, they themselves can estimate the cost implication of design alternatives and can make changes quickly;

(3) everyone in the organization uses the same cost estimates;
(4) the maintenance of such cost tables is relatively easy;
(5) it is not too difficult to link these cost tables to a computer aided design system.

PROCEDURES IN COMPILING COST TABLES

The procedures for compiling a cost table vary depending on whether the cost table is based on the physical product, function, bottom–up or top–down approach. The procedures will be discussed in relation to two different types of cost table.

Physical product using bottom–up approach

The main difficulty with a cost table based on the physical product and using the bottom–up approach is incorporating the plant and machinery details for the machine hour rate (Figure 7.2). After grouping the machines into various categories the following points can be taken into consideration for the machine capacity cost rate:

(1) use replacement cost (and not book value) of machines;
(2) choose depreciation method, such as straight line;
(3) decide depreciation period which should be economic life of machines taking into account both the use of machines (such as 24 hours per day in a three shift system) and expected technological developments;
(4) assume zero salvage value because of technological innovation;
(5) calculate expected preventative maintenance and insurance cost during economic life of machines.

To calculate the operating cost rate for the machine hour rate, the cost of the direct electric power for the machines is required. This is usually estimated by:

average cost per kW × theoretical consumption volume × consumption rate.

The average cost per kW can be estimated from the contract with the electricity company, which will usually show a falling cost per kW as the usage of electricity increases. The theoretical consumption volume can be estimated based on the product specification. The consumption rate is actual consumption volume/theoretical consumption volume. Of course, if necessary the cost of other fuel sources or the cost of water will also be incorporated in the cost table.

The detail included in some cost tables is illustrated by the fact that some companies even calculate the cost of material supplies (such as welding adhesive, oil and thinner) and tool supplies by individual machines. However, it is more common to calculate a material supplies consumption rate based on the expected annual cost of material supplies for each group of machines divided by expected annual operating hours for each group of machines.

For the summary cost table the capacity cost rate and the operating cost rate are calculated per minute of operation for each group of machines and these two rates can be combined to give the machine hour rate. Table 7.1 gives some indication of the grouping of machines and the size of variation in the machine hour rates.

Table 7.1 Extract from cost table by bottom–up method

Equipment	Machine hour rate (yen/min)
Numerically controlled lathe	15.25
Automatic lathe	38.16
Copying lathe	12.71
Vertical milling machine	15.84
Plain milling machine	14.77
Rotary milling machine	23.29
Gear cutter	28.08
Shaving machine	14.51

Function using top–down approach

The procedures for establishing a cost table by the functions of a product using the top–down approach will be discussed for two types of cost table, namely for the basic design and also the detailed design stages of a new product.

Basic design stage

To illustrate the cost table by function using a top–down approach, the example of a small volume product, a conveyor belt, will be used.

Cost table by one variable The length of the conveyor belt has a very significant effect on its cost. Taking the simplest example where only the length of the conveyor belt is known, it has been found that the cost of the conveyor belt can be estimated as a function of its length. Obviously the accuracy of such a cost is only approximate but it has been found to be sufficiently accurate to provide a very useful guide at the basic design stage.

Another example would be the cost of a motor cycle which varies approximately with engine capacity. Simple relationships of this type are both convenient and helpful when new products are at the planning and basic design stages in the product life cycle.

Cost table by multiple regression Returning to the example of the conveyor belt, once other information is available the following estimation function can be used:

$$C = 760 + 16L + 214H + 46N,$$

where C is the cost of the conveyor belt in yen 10 000, L is the length of the conveyor belt in metres, H is horse power in kW and N is the number of curves in the conveyor belt. The above equation has been derived from 29 conveyor belts and this regression equation has proved to be a very good fit in practice, providing an extremely useful basis for estimating cost at the planning and basic design stages.

Detailed design stage

The cost table by function using a top–down approach for the detailed design stage will include more design properties and be more accurate than the cost table for the basic design stage. The steps involved in compiling a cost table at the detailed design stage are given below.

(1) Collect information about functions and design properties of similar products.
(2) Modify past actual cost to be used as future cost
    (a) for internal factors such as:
        (i)   adjust for volume of production,
        (ii) modify fixed cost,
        (iii) adjust for changes in production method or machines;
    (b) for external factors such as:
        (i)   expected price changes,
        (ii) anticipated changes in supply–demand relationship.
(3) Decide final design properties of product.
(4) Establish mathematical function based on relationship between design properties and normal cost data.

As expected at the detailed design stage, more information about the product is available than at the basic design stage. An example of a mass-produced good such as a cogwheel can be used to illustrate such a cost table.

Cost table by multiple regression

In the above example of the conveyor belt at the basic design stage, the cost estimation function took account of three variables, but at the detailed design stage for the cogwheel the production cost can be estimated by:

$$C = -269 + 157M + 11T - 1.7P + 90S + 13W + 268H - 29F - 0.5D,$$

where C is the product cost in yen, M is the model, T is the number of teeth, P is the diameter of the pitch circle (or disk), S is the shift coefficient, W is the width of the teeth, H is the weight of material, F is the weight of the finished part and D

is the diameter of the shaft. This cost estimation function was tested on 30 different cogwheels and the relationship between the product cost and the design properties was found to be close.

Cost table by factor analysis

If even more detail is required it is possible to use a combination of factor analysis and regression with the cost estimation function being based on the design and production process properties for the cogwheel as shown in Table 7.2. In this example of the mass-produced cogwheel, the factor analysis identified three important factors which were incorporated into the cost estimation function:

(1) size of cogwheel;
(2) shape of teeth;
(3) strength.

Table 7.2 Design and production process properties of the cogwheel

Design properties	Process properties
Model	Whether or not it has key seat
Number of teeth	Whether or not it needs shaving
Diameter of pitch circle	
Shift coefficient	Whether or not it needs forging
Width of teeth	Whether or not it needs corner rounding
Weight of material	
Weight of finished part	
Diameter of shaft	

CONCLUSIONS

The above illustrates the great amount of detail included in the cost tables. It should be relatively easy, for example, to estimate the cost of a newly designed cogwheel straight from the cost table without additional work. The cost tables can be held in the form of a database which can be easily amended and updated. Designers and other managers can access the cost tables, although very often with the team approach Japanese management accountants will use the cost tables to answer 'what if?' questions from managers during design team meetings. The compilation of cost tables requires a great deal of work with two or three cost accountants working full-time to maintain the cost tables in a factory with, say, around 6000 employees. However, from the cost management point of view it is possible to compile the less detailed 'top–down' based cost tables relatively easily. Moreover, such top–down cost tables can be particularly helpful in clarifying the important cost relationships and in aiding the design process, particularly during the preparation and basic design stages of a new product. In essence the major change with the cost tables approach is to shift the emphasis from past costs for existing products to future costs for new or redesigned products. Such a change in attitude underlies a contemporary cost management philosophy.

REFERENCES

Sato, R. (1965) *Cost Table*, Sangyou Nouritu Junior College, Japan.

Tamai, M. (1981) *Value Analysis*, Morikita-syupan, Japan.

Tanaka, M. (1986) How to make and use a cost table. *Cost Accounting*, The Japan Cost Accounting Association, No. 20, pp. 35–53.

Tanaka, M. (1988) Cost estimation methods for physical and functional level. *Cost Accounting*, The Japan Cost Accounting Association, No. 2, pp. 41–72.

CHAPTER EIGHT

Activity-based costing: product costs

INTRODUCTION

The initial development of activity-based costing (ABC) in the 1980s was centred on the need to improve product cost information. A series of Harvard Business School cases based on several large US manufacturing firms indicated that similar steps were being taken to refine the ways in which overheads were being unitized in order to provide a new perspective on product line profitability. Professors Cooper and Kaplan of Harvard coined the term ABC as a title for this approach and were instrumental in formalizing, developing and publicizing ABC. Their success in this respect is reflected in the growth of research and publications on ABC, on its adoption as an approach by many leading accountancy consultancies and from the interest which it has engendered among management accounting practitioners.

THE 'TRADITIONAL' PROBLEM

Historically, overhead costs have been attached to individual products in proportion to the direct labour (production worker) time and/or the machine time spent on them. The validity of these practices rests on the existence of a reasonably close correlation between the incurrence of overhead costs and the level of labour and machine hours. Clearly this will be the case if overheads are related to production time (e.g. lighting costs) or machining time (e.g. machine power). Moreover as both labour and machine time are closely related to the volume of production undertaken by the firm, these two common bases of overhead absorption are ultimately based on the notion that production volume is the predominant cause of production overhead. While the assumption may have had a widespread validity in the past it is unrealistic for many modern manufacturing businesses. One reason has been a shrinkage in direct labour often to relatively insignificant levels (e.g. under 5% of production costs in many electronics companies) which has resulted in massive overhead rates, often expressed as over 1000% of labour. The scope for error using such a small cost element to act as a basis for the allocation of costs which dwarf it so comprehensively has therefore increased substantially. Another factor detracting from labour or machine time as an explanation of overhead cost has been the increase in the existence of flexible manufacturing systems, multiple component parts, total quality policies and of a diversity of often customized outputs which has created the demand for resources which are influenced by the extent of a whole range of activities and not simply by the number of units produced. Miller and Vollman (1985) have summarized into four categories the type of activities or transactions which give rise to many of the significant overheads in contemporary manufacturing operations.

(1) Logistical transactions. Activities involving the order execution and confirmation of the movement of materials within the factory. These activities ensure materials are tracked, recorded and analysed.

(2) Balancing transactions. Activities aimed at ensuring that the supply of production resources is arranged to meet the demands of work obtained by the firm. These activities ensure that the instructions and authorizations for logistical transactions are issued.

(3) Quality transactions. Activities aimed at ensuring the quality requirements of the firm are being met. These acti-

vities include the setting of specifications in production and procurement procedures aimed at meeting and checking specifications and the maintenance of relevant records.
(4) Change transactions. Activities which are aimed at dealing with changes in product design, work schedules and material specifications. These activities represent the continuous effort expended to ensure that the firm reacts effectively and efficiently to deviations from expectations.

Transactions of these four types will account for significant and growing proportions of overhead cost in the contemporary factory. The need for activities such as these is the main reason why overhead cost has increased its relative importance as a component of production cost. However, the resources which have to be committed to them, and hence their cost, are influenced by factors other than production volume. The transactions involved, for example the number of material movements, the number of material orders, the number of inspections and the number of schedule revisions, reflect the range, diversity, complexity and quality of output rather than simply its volume.

Furthermore, non-production overheads comprising mainly selling, marketing and distribution costs have commonly been attached to individual products as a standard percentage add-on to production cost. This practice ignores differences, unrelated to production cost, in the resources committed to and effort expended on selling individual products. It also ignores the fact that the same product may be marketed in different ways in different markets and distributed through different distribution channels to different customers.

Thus the whole area of overhead costing is one which can, through the use of these conventional and convenient procedures, result in unit product costs which do not accurately reflect the resources which have been consumed by the existence of that product. Where overheads are relatively large and have significant non-volume driven components the problem will be most serious. The potential for misleading product cost information to be provided systematically to management in situations like these is therefore clear.

ACTIVITY-BASED COSTING

Activity-based costing (ABC), occasionally referred to as trans-actions costing, provides a methodology which can address these problems. It is based on the basic premises that:

(1) activities consume resources and
(2) products consume activities.

On this basis the structure of ABC product costing (Figure 8.1) is founded. First the major overhead activities are identified and it is these activities rather than the production depart-ments in a traditional system (see Figure 3.4) which provide the basis for pooling overhead costs.

Identification of activities will frequently cross the functional organization chart, e.g. procurement activity may occur in buying, finance, administration sections and delivery sections, or maintenance activity may occur through all production de-partments. Interviews with managers to ascertain how capital and labour resources are used in the overhead areas of the firm with possible supplementation by self-analysis returns by staff will provide the basic data from which the costs are pooled into the selected activities. At these stages the level of detail of

Stage 1: Activity identification

Stage 2: Attribution of cost to activities

Stage 3: Identification and measurement of cost driver (association of drivers with product lines)

Stage 4: Calculation of cost driver rates

Stage 5; Application of cost driver rates

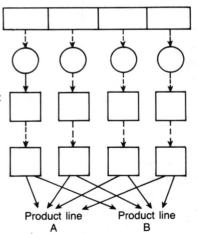

Product line A   Product line B

Figure 8.1 The structure of activity-based costing in a production facility.

the system is established through the selection of the number of cost pools. For product costing purposes each activity cost pool should be as homogeneous as possible, i.e. the pooled costs all closely relate to the one chosen cost driver. The cost driver will be a measure which reflects the volume of work undertaken within an activity for the firm's product lines. Table 8.1 shows the typical types of pool and cost driver which exist in some of the reported cases of ABC.

Table 8.1 Examples of activity cost pools and cost drivers

Activity cost pool	Cost driver
Set-up	Number of set-ups or set-up minutes
Quality control	Number of inspections
Procurement	Number of suppliers or number of purchase orders
Customer liaison	Number of customers/location of departments Number of customer orders
Materials handling	Number of material movements/distance of moves

In practice, the cost drivers used have tended to be one of three types.

(1) Situational quantification. For example, the number of customers or suppliers existing for an organization. These underlie the work load level of the respective activities relating to these parties.

(2) Activity work volume. For example, the number of customer orders or the number of purchase orders which represent the work output of the respective activities.

(3) Activity work volume/complexity. Where the work volume drivers are not themselves reasonably homogeneous in respect of their consumption of the activities resources then they may be weighted to reflect the factor which causes this non-homogeneity. For example, the location of a supplier or a customer may affect the work which goes into producing or meeting an order. Weighting the orders by location may therefore provide a weighted volume-

based cost driver which will produce a more realistic attachment of the respective costs to product lines [see Innes and Mitchell (1991) for a detailed example].

The cost driver provides the denominator for the computation of a rate for each activity. One other prerequisite of the cost driver is that it can be clearly associated with each individual product line. This is necessary in order to apply the rate to each product and so achieve the object of the whole process: product line costings. ABC can also be applied to non-production overheads [see for example Cooper and Kaplan (1991) which deals with distribution cost] where the units sold rather than the units produced will be the focus for costing. In these instances costs may be influenced not simply by the product but by the distribution channel used, the customer requirement and possibly even the location of the sale. These issues are explored in more detail in Chapter 9.

STRUCTURING THE ABC SYSTEM

While the above outline reflects the basis of ABC and mirrors the first reported instances of ABC, some further refinements of how an ABC product costing system might be more beneficially structured have been suggested by Cooper (1992). This approach involves the recognition that costs are 'driven' at different levels of activity within an organization. For example, some production costs will be primarily influenced by the number of units (e.g. direct material) of output produced while others will be determined by the number of product lines in the range offered (e.g. product manager's salary). ABC costings may therefore be reported in a manner which will indicate not only the ingredients of total cost but also the level at which the cost is driven. Cooper (1992) suggests four levels will commonly be found in practice.

(1) Unit level activities. These are performed each time a unit is produced and they consume an amount of resource which is fairly similar for each unit. Examples of costs

falling into this category would include direct labour, direct material, machine power and depreciation.

(2) Batch level activities. These are performed each time a batch of products is processed. The consumption of resources is reflected in the selected cost drivers associated with each batch. Examples of costs falling into this category would include the cost of process set-up, batch inspection and material handling and movement.

(3) Product level activities. These are performed to sustain the existence of a particular product line. Here cost drivers relate to the consumption of resources by the product line category. Examples of costs falling into this category include customer liaison, purchasing and part administration and product specifications.

(4) Facility level activities. These are performed to sustain the general production capability of a manufacturing plant. These activities are of a level normally so divorced from individual products to make any cost unitization highly tenuous and arbitrary. Examples of costs falling into this category include plant management, light and heat and property occupancy.

These four levels provide a structure for computing and reporting costs on an ABC basis. It is, however, a structure which might be amended to take account of the particular nature of costs in an individual firm. For example, in some firms a production line or production process or a product grouping (instead of a single product) might provide other hierarchical levels for cost analysis. One significant benefit of this approach over conventional costing is that it emphasizes that costs are influenced or driven by a variety of factors. Some will certainly vary with volume but many others, conventionally classified simply as fixed, will vary with the number of batches produced or the range and diversity of products produced, or indeed the number of production facilities used. This type of analysis therefore highlights for management the way costs behave in their organization. It provides a considerable enhancement on the traditional simple and unrealistic two-way split of costs into fixed and variable categories. Thus as well as providing more accurate product costs ABC can provide a foundation for improving cost information for decision making and cost management (see Chapter 9).

An example

Table 8.2 provides an example of how this structured ABC approach contrasts with the traditional approach to costing. Aside from the more detailed information provided on overheads through the use of multiple cost driver rates, the product costs produced under the ABC approach differ from those obtained more conventionally. In particular, respective unit costs of product A and product C contrast markedly. In the case of the former, high volume, basic product the unit cost is almost halved while the latter specialist, small batch product shows a unit cost around three and a half times the conventionally determined cost. In effect the labour cost basis has resulted in product A subsidizing product C. It is only when the consumption of overhead (which is a large element of cost) by each product is reflected more accurately through identifying its high demand for set-ups, inspections, etc., that this is apparent. Indeed the example is typical of the type of results which ABC systems have been producing in practice: small batch, complex products having their costs upgraded significantly to the benefit of the more routine, large volume products.

Table 8.2 Traditional costing versus ABC

I. DATA

Product output:

  Product A: A long established product, produced in large production runs of 10 000 units to be held in stock to await customer orders. Annual production 120 000 units.

  Product B: A customized version of product A made to order in small batches of 100 units. Annual production 60 000 units.

  Product C: A new and complex product manufactured in batches of 10. Annual production 12 000 units.

Table 8.2 *(continued)*

Production costs:

	Product A £'000s	Product B £'000s	Product C £'000s
Direct material	600	360	96
Direct labour	240	120	36
Production overhead	1200	600	180
	2040	1080	312

Production overhead:

The above costing attaches production overhead to each product on the basis of direct labour cost (at a rate of 500%). The production overhead comprises the following costs.

	£'000s
Indirect labour	
Set-up supervision/work	320
Material handling	280
Inspection staff	200
Procurement staff	210
Production specification staff	100
Plant management	160
Other costs	
Heat and light	80
Building occupancy	190
Material handling equipment depreciation	80
Machine power	140
Supplies (inspection)	70
Supplies (procurement)	60
Supplies (product specification)	40
Supplies (general management)	50
	1980

Cost driver data:

Machine time per unit for the products is in the ratio:
  product A: 1
  product B: 1.5
  product C: 3.5

Set-ups of a standard type are required for each batch run.

Standard inspections are undertaken for each batch on the basis:
  product A: 50 units in each batch
  product B: 5 units in each batch

(continued)

Table 8.2 (*continued*)

product C: 2 units in each batch
Material movements required for each batch:
  product A: 25
  product B: 50
  product C: 100
Purchase orders required for each product:
  product A: 200 orders
  product B: 400 orders
  product C: 1400 orders
Product specifications maintained for each product:
  product A: 50
  product B: 75
  product C: 200

II. COSTING RESULTS
Traditional product costing results

| | Unit cost | | |
	Product A (£)	Product B (£)	Product C (£)
Direct material	5.00	6.00	8.00
Direct labour	2.00	2.00	3.00
Production overhead	10.00	10.00	15.00
Total unit cost	17.00	18.00	26.00

ABC results (see below for workings)

| | Product A | | Product B | | Product C | |
	£ (total)	£ (per unit)	£ (total)	£ (per unit)	£ (total)	£ (per unit)
Unit level:						
Direct material	600 000	5.00	360 000	6.00	96 000	8.00
Direct labour	240 000	2.00	120 000	2.00	36 000	3.00
Machine power (rounded)	66 700	0.56	50 000	0.83	23 300	1.94
	906 700	7.56	530 000	8.83	155 300	12.94

Table 8.2 *(continued)*

Batch level:						
Inspection (£45 per insp.)	27 000	0.23	135 000	2.25	108 000	9.00
Material handling (£2.40 per material movement)	720	0.01	72 000	1.20	288 000	24.00
Set-up (£176. 60 per set-up)	2120	0.02	105 960	1.77	211 920	17.66
	29 840	0.26	312 960	5.22	607 920	50.66
Product level:						
Procurement (£135 per order)	27 000	0.23	54 000	0.90	189 000	15.75
Product specification (£430.77 per specification)	21 540	0.18	32 310	0.54	86 150	7.18
	48 540	0.41	86 310	1.44	275 150	22.93
Facility level:						
General management (heat, light and occupancy costs)	277 200	2.31	158 400	2.64	43 560	3.63
Total unit cost	1 262 280	10.54	1 087 670	18.13	1 081 930	90.16

ABC workings

Unit level – Direct material and labour as per conventional system.
     – Machine power is allocated to product line on the basis of the ratio computed below.

	Volume	Ratio of usage	Total
Product A	120 000	1	120 000
Product B	60 000	1.5	90 000
Product C	12 000	3.5	42 000
			252 000

Rate $= \dfrac{£140\,000}{£252\,000} = £0.56$ per weighted volume unit

(continued)

Table 8.2 *(continued)*

Batch level – Inspection on the basis of number inspections.

	No. of Batches	Inspections per batch	No. of inspections
Product A	12	50	600
Product B	600	5	3000
Product C	1200	2	2400
			6000

Inspection cost (£): Staff   200 000
                    Supplies   70 000
                                270 000

$$\text{Rate for costing} = \frac{£270\,000}{6000} = £45.00 \text{ per inspection}$$

– Material handling on the basis of material movements.

	No. of batches	Material movements per batch	No. of material movements
Product A	12	25	300
Product B	600	50	30 000
Product C	1200	100	120 000
			150 300

Material handling cost (£): Staff   280 000
                          Depreciation   80 000
                                         360 000

$$\text{Rate for costing} = \frac{£360\,000}{150\,300} = £2.40 \text{ per material}$$
movement

– Set-up on the basis of number of set-ups.

No. of set-ups (1 per batch)	
Product A	12
Product B	600
Product C	1200
	1812

Set-up cost (£): Staff   320 000

$$\text{Rate for costing} = \frac{£320\,000}{1812} = £176.60 \text{ per set-up}$$

Product level – Procurement on the basis of purchase orders.

Table 8.2 *(continued)*

	No. of purchase orders
Product A	200
Product B	400
Product C	1400
	2000

Procurement cost (£):	Staff	210 000
	Supplies	60 000
		270 000

Rate for costing $= \dfrac{£270\,000}{£2000} = £135.00$ per order

– Product specification on the basis of number of maintained specifications.

	No. of specifications
Product A	50
Product B	75
Product C	200
	325

Product spec. costs (£):	Staff	100 000
	Supplies	40 000
		140 000

Rate for costing $= \dfrac{£140\,00}{£325} = £430.77$ per specification

Facility level – Allocated to products on the basis of prime cost (direct material + direct labour)

	Prime cost per unit (£)	Units produced (£)	Total price cost (£)
Product A	7.00	120 000	840 000
Product B	8.00	60 000	480 000
Product C	11.00	12 000	132 000
			1 452 000

Facility costs (£):	Staff	160 000
	Heat and light	80 000
	Occupancy	190 000
	Supplies	50 000
		480 000

Rate for costing $= \dfrac{£480\,000}{1\,452\,000} = £0.33$ per £ of prime cost

ABC AND THE SERVICE SECTOR

The ABC approach is just as applicable to the service industry as manufacturing. Although there are markedly fewer reported instances of ABC being applied in this sector a number of examples have been identified in a range of publications by Rotch (1990), who outlines railroad, hospital, data management applications, and Cooper and Kaplan (1991), who have produced railroad, bank and hospital cases. Further examples in the financial services sector have been identified in a UK survey (Innes and Mitchell, 1991) and the application of ABC in banking has been described by Sephton and Ward (1990). The design of ABC systems for service organizations typically involves the following steps. First, the work carried out by staff and equipment has to be arranged into activities. This is normally achieved by a combination of interview and self-analysis by the staff and management involved. As with the manufacturing firm, activities selected may well cut across the conventional (usually functional) organization structure and will be based on a grouping of work types which are as homogeneous as possible in respect of their output. The output when measured will provide the cost driver which can be used to associate the cost with a cost object. This will mean that end-services (the ultimate source of demand for activities) will have the cost of activities traced to them. This process is outlined in Figure 8.2.

Each activity's output should be traceable to the source of the demand for it. Where the object is to cost a service provided to external customers then tracing the output directly to this cost object will best meet this aim. However, it should be recognized that direct links of this type might not always exist where, for example, one activity is providing a service for another activity rather than for the end-service. Here a system of cross activity charging may have to be instituted in order to obtain a cost system which reflects how resources are actually being used.

Abstracting (and simplifying) from the hospital cases of Rotch (1990) and Cooper and Kaplan (1991) it is possible to

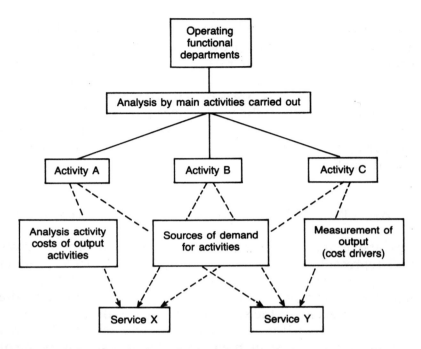

Figure 8.2 The activity-based costing process in service costing.

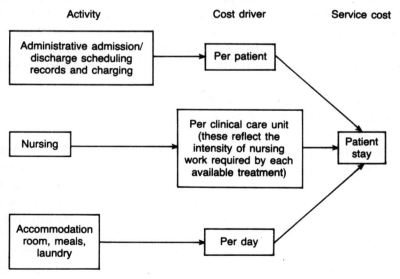

Figure 8.3 An outline structure of activity-based costing in a hospital.

show an outline of an ABC system for a service sector business. The system contrasts with the prior approach which was to charge a standard average rate per day as a basis for the costing of a patient's treatment. Under an ABC regime this was charged to reflect three areas of activity which each represent one constituent part of the total service (Figure 8.3). A separate costing rate for each, reflecting that activities' cost driver, produces a cost which reflects more accurately the use of resources by each patient.

ASSESSING ACTIVITY-BASED PRODUCT AND SERVICE COSTS

The above analysis shows how activity-based product costs will represent an extension of marginal or variable product costing to include those overheads which, although not varying directly with production volume, will be influenced by the nature and extent of the support activities of the organization. Indeed, where facility level costs are included then the final outputs of the ABC system will be full unit costs. The value of this information must be judged against the purpose to which it is put. In most published cases of ABC the new product costs have been compared with selling prices to provide an analysis of product line profitability. Frequently the results have shown that a small number of products generate a disproportionately large amount of the firm's total profits. In addition, the systematic biases of conventional full costing (subsidization of small, variable batch production by large volume products) have been shown up. Traditional analysis of the worth of individual product lines has rested on the application of contribution (selling price less variable cost) analysis. Advocates of ABC argue that this provides only a limited and short-term perspective for management as all costs, other than those which are purely volume driver, are assumed to remain fixed. The fixity of cost depends upon both the time perspective taken (all costs can be altered in the long-term) and the fact that, for example, dropping a product line would impact on activities at both the batch and product as well as unit level.

Therefore, an ABC computation of product cost and product line profitability will give a better indication of how costs might change with alterations to product range and mix. This is achieved by linking the decision to its impact on activities and so the resource consumption. In other words, the ABC approach brings to the attention of management the best measure of long-term variable cost (Johnson and Kaplan, 1987) and is therefore particularly suitable for use in strategic decision-making involving the product portfolio. For example, the consideration of specialization in high volume/large batch production might be indicated in some situations. The ABC analysis of product line costs and profitability thus provides an attention-directing mechanism for management. It can be used as a basis in the categorization of products for policy assessment (Table 8.3). This type of analysis can highlight a longer term perspective than (variable costing based) contribution, where product volume might be increased or decreased, where more promotion is worthwhile, where selling price might be amended, where components are best bought-in rather than made in-house, and those which might be dropped completely.

Table 8.3 Product profitability analysis

Low volume/high profit Possible policy: promote	High volume/high profit Possible policy: foster and protect
Low volume/low profit Possible policy: discontinue	High volume/low profit Possible policy: internal cost reduction

It should, of course, be borne in mind that the most appropriate information for these types of decisions is an analysis of the future spending and revenue (i.e. cash flow) implications which would result from them. Three aspects of ABC limit its relevance in this respect. First, historic product cost, even on an ABC basis, does not provide this information. It provides information only on past costs and would only give direct guidance on the future if the past circumstances were to continue, i.e. the business is operating in a static environment. Changes in technology, organization, inflation, etc., make this most unlikely. However, the past can provide a basis for future estimation and ABC provides a much more detailed basis for this in respect of its more detailed treatment of overheads and its identification of cost causality through the gathering and reporting of cost driver data. Second, the existence of joint costs means that the cost of one product cannot be satisfactorily isolated from that of others. For example, a cost driver may pertain to more than one product. Thus a purchase order or a set-up could be common to both products A and B and the dropping of A might not therefore reduce the activity consumption as measured by that cost driver. Third, the costs reported for products in an ABC system represent the cost of resources consumed by the product. While dropping the product may curtail consumption of these resources, the cash flow implications may be less immediate. For example, depreciation of equipment, a cost which does not have current cash flow implications, may be included in the cost. Its elimination would not reduce spending (see Chapter 2). Also, the saving of only portions of worker time may simply create some idle time rather than allowing a reduction in the labour force.

ABC product costs do provide a more detailed and refined treatment of overheads. Advocates claim a more realistic result and one which provides a sounder basis for setting and assessing selling prices, for ascertaining product mix and in particular taking 'make or buy' and product discontinuance decisions. These benefits stem from the improvements which it encompasses in respect of linking costs to the cost object in a manner which actually reflects cost causality and so provides insight into how these costs really behave. This style of understanding provides a keystone of cost management.

REFERENCES

Cooper, R. (1992) Activity based costing for improved product costing, in *Handbook of Cost Management* (ed. B. J. Brinker), Warren Gorham and Lamont, Boston, pp. B1-1 to B1-50.

Cooper, R. and Kaplan, R.S. (1991) *The Design of Cost Management Systems*, Prentice Hall, Englewood Cliffs, New Jersey.

Innes, J. and Mitchell, F. (1991) *Activity Based Cost Management: a case study of development and implementation*, CIMA.

Johnson, H.T. and Kaplan, R.S. (1987) The importance of long-term product costs. *The McKinsey Quarterly*, Autumn, 36–48.

Miller, J.G. and Vollman, T.E. (1985) The hidden factory. *Harvard Business Review*, September/October, **63**, 142–50.

Rotch, W. (1990) Activity based costing in service industries. *Journal of Cost Management*, Summer, **4**(2), 4–14.

Sephton, M. and Ward, T. (1990) ABC in retail financial services. *Management Accounting (UK)*, April, **68**(4), 29 and 33.

CHAPTER NINE

Activity-based cost management

INTRODUCTION

Although it was the pursuit of more accurate product cost information which led to the initial development of activity-based costing (ABC) systems during the latter half of the 1980s it soon became apparent that the potential of this approach to costing extended well beyond this single narrow objective. Many other uses of ABC, perhaps even more central to cost management than product costing, evolved as firms, consultants and academics explored and developed the novel information generated by their ABC analysis. This chapter examines and assesses a range of these further applications of the ABC approach.

COST VISIBILITY

ABC can generate information which provides a detailed perspective on how overhead resources have been used within a firm. Rather than the normal accounting analysis which usually categorizes these expenses in accord with the type of resource acquired, e.g. salaries, stationery, heating, transport, etc., the ABC approach provides an analysis of how these resources were used. By so doing the costs are linked to the activities which have caused them. This serves two managerial purposes. First, it provides an indication of why the costs were

Table 9.1 Customer order processing

	£'000s
Conventional analysis[a]	
Salaries	290
Office equipment depreciation	84
Travel and accommodation	158
Stationery and office supplies	31
Telephone	29
	592
ABC analysis	
Vetting of customers (credit worthiness, etc.)	90
Order taking	114
Customer agreements	38
Quotations and pricing	105
Customer liaison	91
Problem/error resolution	84
Expediting	70
	592

[a] Even this analysis would probably require a one-off exercise to ascertain the costs incurred in each department involved, e.g. customer liaison, finance, admininstration, goods receiving, etc.

incurred and therefore allows management to assess whether the purpose merits the cost associated with its pursuit. Second, it links cost to cause and to the individuals with responsibility for the consumption of resources giving rise to the cost. This guides managerial attention to the cost source where action must be directed if control is to be exercised effectively.

Table 9.1 provides an example of how an ABC analysis of the purchasing overhead would contrast with a more conventional cost analysis. Often, for the first time, the ABC analysis will gather together the costs of an activity which crosses existing departmental boundaries. It therefore provides management with new information on the relative commitment of resources within the overhead area. This information alone has frequently proved to be 'surprising' to management (Innes and Mitchell, 1990; Develin *et al.*, 1990) and has provided a basis for targeting and prioritizing cost reduction efforts. However, the subdivision of the activity into its constituent parts is of no less importance. This requires the accountant to, first, become familiar with what is done within the particular area of activity being analysed. Subactivities of the type which comprise order processing (Table 9.1) are usually identified from interviews with experienced staff working in the area. The level of detail to which the analysis is taken at this stage is a matter of judgement for the accountants and managers concerned with the design of the system. Some of the factors relevant to this aspect of the analysis include the following.

(1) The importance of the activity in terms of its cost. Where, for example, the cost of an activity is relatively immaterial its cost may be immersed in that of a larger related one. For feedback purposes all activities of significance in their own right in cost terms should be identified separately. Moreover, where an activity has a history of cost growth there is a strong case that can be made for its inclusion in the analysis as a separate item.

(2) Where the organization wishes to operate on the basis of responsibility accounting then the subactivity analysis may be designed to match areas of managerial authority.

(3) Particularly where the system is geared to product costing then activities should be selected such that each activity cost pool is relatively homogeneous in the sense that the selected cost driver can legitimately be used as an explanation of the cost.

COST ANALYSIS

The increased visibility which ABC provides through its profiling of overhead cost by activities and subactivities provides a basis for a range of additional types of cost analysis.

Cost reporting

The initial profile of the costs of each activity provides management with information on the extent to which resources have been committed to different purposes. This may be reviewed against the relative importance which management attributes to these activities. Variations between the two may indicate areas targeted either for extra resources or cut-backs. The cost per activity figures also provides another basis for monitoring trends in cost over time. In this way the sources of overhead cost growth can be pin-pointed for management. Finally, this information which is task oriented provides a basis for intra-, and where information can be obtained, inter-firm comparisons. The cost aspect of the performance of activities can be compared among different plants and subsidiaries with the aim of disseminating information on how particularly efficient performance has been achieved so that others can adopt a similar approach.

Value-added analysis

The variety of costed activities generated by ABC provides a basis for management to assess each one in terms of the value and necessity of the contribution which it makes to the organization. One popular means of doing this is to screen each in order to decide whether or not it adds value to the business. In a literal sense the value added by a business is represented by the sales value of its output (i.e. what its customers were willing to pay for the output) less the bought-in goods and services which contributed to the final outputs (Morley, 1978). This difference represents the wealth (or value added) created specifically by the producing firm for its investors, employees and lenders. If activities undertaken within the firm are not essential to the generation of this wealth then from an economic or financial perspective the commitment of resources to them may be questioned. Their elimination provides no diminution of the value placed on the organization's output by its customers and the resultant cost reduction increases the wealth available to investors, employees and lenders.

The real problems of applying this analysis lie in identifying the non-value-added work which exists in an organization. ABC provides a starting point by providing management with

Table 9.2 Value-added (VA) activity analysis

Activity	Assessment
Receive materials	VA
Check against order	VA?
Notify administration	VA?
Unpack materials	VA?
Store materials	VA?
Issue and move materials	VA?
Record issue	VA?
Deal with administration queries	VA?
Identifying and dispose of damaged materials	VA?

information on what is being done and on the amount of the related costs. Table 9.2 lists a series of activities related to materials handling.

The receipt of materials is clearly one necessary activity within a production organization. However, each of the subsequent activities might be questioned, to differing degrees, as to whether or not they add value in the business (Table 9.3).

Clearly there is some dubiety about the value-added/non-value-added categorization of many activities. The acid test is to ask,

Can we provide at least the same customer value if this activity no longer existed?

For many of the activities in Table 9.3 the answer would be yes, contingent upon other changes being made in the organization. For example, the elimination of stock would only result in no loss of customer value if just-in-time (JIT) procedures could be established. Thus an activity may often be value-added in the short-term but not in the longer-term when accommodating change is possible. However, the analysis, and simply the focus it gives on what is done in the organization is valuable to management and certainly raises issues and directs attention in meaningful ways.

One other caveat to the value-added approach lies in the potential risks associated with the pursuit of value added as ctivities and value added

	Value added?
Check against order	This may not be considered necessary if complete supplier reliability is established.
Notify administration/record	Again the firm's effectiveness to produce saleable output without detailed administrative procedures might render these activities questionable as directly adding value.
Unpack material	If material could be received in a conveniently usable form then this activity could be eliminated. It only adds value because of the current mode of delivery.
Store materials	Storing and the existence of stocks or inventories can be viewed as non-value added as efficient organization on a JIT basis may remove the need for such activities. However, where such organization is made impossible, perhaps through supplier limitations, one might argue that stocking does add value through assisting in the achievement of out-time deliveries to customers.
Issue and move materials	This activity may be at least partially avoided if the factory can be arranged such that supplier deliveries are made direct to the production line and therefore it can be considered as non-value added.
Dealing with queries/disposal of damaged materials	Both activities are functions of inefficiencies in the system and can therefore be considered non-value added.

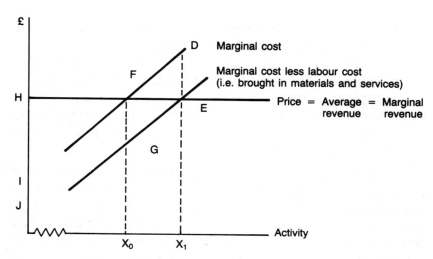

Figure 9.1 Value-added maximization.

an objective of the business. Value added does not equate to profit and if it becomes the main focus of the business it can lead to suboptimization with respect to profit (Figure 9.1). Assume that the firm is a price taker with no fixed costs. A unit marginal cost which eventually rises would lead to a profit maximizing output at X_0 with profit FHI. If, however, value added is maximized then this would happen at X_1 with a total value added of EHJ. At this level however the profit would be FHI less DEF, i.e. the maximization of value added has cost the firm profits of DEF.

While certain activities (from X_0 to X_1) add value they also add a labour cost which exceeds it and so reduces profit. Thus, where this type of analysis is being applied in the assessment of activities within the firm, labour cost should be identified and reported so that full marginal cost, and hence the profit impact of activity changes, can be recognized.

Core, support, discretionary analysis

Another similar approach to the assessment of activities (Bellis-Jones and Hand, 1989) categorizes them in terms of whether they are:

(1) core – the purpose for which the activity exists, e.g. the preparation of a report by an accountant;

(2) support – required in order to make the core activity possible, e.g. the accountant ordering paper for the report or typing the report;

(3) discretionary – caused by deficiencies in the system, e.g. the accountant correcting data wrongly computed for inclusion in the report.

This type of analysis will reveal to management the real cost of inadequacies (discretionary activity cost) within the organization and indicate the extent to which employees are diverted (through both support and discretionary activities) from achieving their core objectives. Such attention-directing information can then lead to a more effective arrangement of activities.

BUDGETING AND VARIANCE ANALYSIS

Traditional budgeting and standard costing produces overhead variances which have been subject to two major criticisms. First, the computation of variances is, as in most conventional costing systems, based upon the use of volume-related overhead absorption bases such as labour hours or machine hours (Solomons, 1968). Flexing the budget on the basis of these variables produces relatively meaningless values for what cost 'should be' and hence renders the resultant variances of questionable utility. Second, the computation of a total standard cost of fixed overhead involves treating these fixed costs as if they were variable (Horngren, 1967) and again results in a devaluation of the worth of the cost variances.

ABC, when applied in this area, provides a methodology which can contribute to the rectification of these difficulties. The use of a range of cost drivers provides a refinement which when applied to a series of appropriate standard cost driver rates will generate a more accurate measure of the expected overhead cost. Table 9.4 shows how a traditional variable overhead spending variance would contrast with the ABC approach. An apparently favourable variance of £2000 becomes an unfavourable variance of £950. In addition, the ABC approach provides more detail on how the variance came about, allowing management to pin-point its source among the three categories of overhead. Clearly, this approach does not simply assume overhead will vary with a single, volume-correlated measure. It treats overhead as being a function of how production will influence set-ups, inspections and material movements.

Table 9.4 Variance analysis and ABC

Traditional
Data:

Standard rate	£10 per direct labour hour
Standard allowance	2 direct labour hours per unit
Actual spend	£22 000
Actual direct labour hours	2400

Variances:

Actual	Actual hours
	×
	standard rate
	2400 hours
	×
	£10
£22 000	= £24 000

Spending
variance
£2000F

ABC
Data:

Standard cost driver rates	£100 per set-up
	£5 per inspection
	£4 per material move
Actual cost drivers	110 set-ups
	1050 inspections
	1200 material moves
Actual spend	£11 500 on set-up
	£5800 on quality control
	£4700 on material handling

(continued)

Table 9.4 *(continued)*

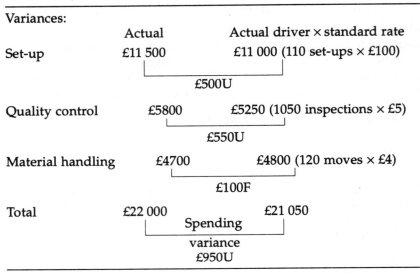

Variances:	Actual	Actual driver × standard rate
Set-up	£11 500	£11 000 (110 set-ups × £100)
		£500U
Quality control	£5800	£5250 (1050 inspections × £5)
		£550U
Material handling	£4700	£4800 (120 moves × £4)
		£100F
Total	£22 000	£21 050
	Spending	
	variance	
	£950U	

One further benefit of the ABC approach would come from incorporating the original budget into the analysis. Suppose this had been set on the basis of the capacity available in each overhead area at 120 set-ups, 1100 inspections and 1500 material movements. As shown in Table 9.5, the budget profiles the capacity available in terms of each cost driver. Actual wage usage shows how much of this has been utilized in the period, so giving the variances representing unused capacity. The information may be provided in non-financial terms (as above) or in cost terms by applying the standard cost driver rates to the activity volumes. Management is provided with an indication of how much of the resource provided in each area has been used. The resultant identification of potential spare ca-

Table 9.5 Capacity usage

	Budget capacity	Actual usage	Variance
Set-ups	120	110	(10)
Inspections	1100	1050	(50)
Material movements	1500	1200	(300)

pacity can direct managerial attention to overhead areas where cost reduction might be considered or to bottlenecks where some extra resource might be needed.

Finally, the utilization of multiple cost drivers can provide a valuable starting point for the setting of budgets in the overhead area. By estimating cost driver volumes in these areas a previously absent justification for expected cost levels is available to management. If these variables are chosen to represent each area's demand for resources then increases or decreases in them can provide the basis of a case for raising or reducing the budget. Rather than simply allowing for inflation the budgeting process automatically requires an examination of the underlying need for funds in each overhead area.

INFLUENCING BEHAVIOUR

One might argue that management accounting exists to influence and change behaviour beneficially within an organization. A management accounting system which is ignored or which misleads is of questionable value. One of the main attributes of an ABC system is its ability to clearly deliver costing information in a way which does impact upon managerial decisions. This occurs principally through its focus upon cost driver information and the appreciation of cost behaviour which it promotes. Several instances have already been noted (Innes and Mitchell, 1990) of accountants reporting on much improved communication of cost information when ABC is used. Improved understanding and acceptance of cost data by management was apparent and their increased involvement with costing was visible in their use of the information to direct questions, suggest improvements and make decisions.

Thus, the choice of cost drivers can be of fundamental importance in terms of influencing behaviour. Indeed, Hiromoto (1988) suggests that in Japan direct labour hours are commonly used as the basis for overhead absorption (in the knowledge that the results will lack costing accuracy) in order to motivate designers to automate production and design labour out of new products. A similar approach was taken within an ABC framework by the US corporation Tektronix (Jonez and Wright, 1987). Their problem also related to new product design with designers proliferating the use of new components from new suppliers when in many instances it was felt that more standard, already used parts would also have been appropriate. This was identified as the root cause of growth in material-related overhead. The Tektronix accountants who had adopted the ABC approach decided to focus attention on this issue and try to change designer behaviour by channelling all of the material-related overhead to products through one cost driver. Table 9.6 illustrates how this was done. The overhead attaches to each part used by the designers and clearly penalizes the use of parts which are not already used in the large volume products. Combined with the establishment of target product costs for the designers these rates provide strong motivation to make use of parts already in high usage by the company. This avoids the administrative cost of carrying yet another part number, of vetting and liaising with another supplier and of ironing out the inevitable teething problems which occur when new materials are used. Tektronix found that this costing change had a significant impact on their designers' cost consciousness in this area.

Table 9.6 Tektronix cost driver rate

	Material overhead:	£10 million
	No. of active parts:	8000
Therefore, annual 'carrying' cost of part:		$\dfrac{£10\,\text{million}}{8000} = £1250$
Assume typical	high usage part is used 40 000 times per annum	
	low usage part is used 40 times per annum	
Thus the cost driver rates are:		
	Rate (high usage part)	$\dfrac{£1250}{40\,000} = £0.03125$
	Rate (low usage part)	$\dfrac{£1250}{40} = £31.25$

PERFORMANCE MEASUREMENT

Johnson (1988) has emphasized the contribution which ABC can make to day-to-day operational control through the regular reporting of cost driver volumes. Together these provide a package of non-financial performance indicators on the level of work undertaken in many areas of activity within an organization. As these measures are non-financial they can normally be more quickly prepared and fed-back to managers and their meaning is easily understood. In addition, it has the advantage of creating a clear focus on activities rather than costs. According to Johnson, it is activities rather than simply costs which can be managed most directly and effectively. The cost driver measures are fundamental indicators of the effort being made in the support areas of the business process. They show where more effort is being expended (e.g. more inspections), where effort is slackening off (e.g. less set-ups) and where potential waste is occurring (e.g. more material movements). Operational management can use this in day-to-day use of resources and longer-term trends-apparent to top management, may lead to more permanent re-allocations of resources.

Performance measurement is one area where some care has to be taken in applying ABC because it is often the case that you 'get what you measure'. If employees take cost driver volumes as the main measures of their performance they may be motivated to increase the number of set-ups, inspections or orders which they make in a period. This behaviour will defeat the purpose of the costing system as these factors drive cost and will increase it. The inclusion of cost information in the measure in the form of a cost driver rate will not necessarily alleviate this problem

$$\frac{\text{cost}}{\text{cost driver}} = \text{rate reduced by} \begin{array}{l} \text{(1) reducing cost and/or} \\ \text{(2) increasing driver volume.} \end{array}$$

As shown in Table 9.6, one means of reducing the cost driver rate is to increase the denominator, or cost driver volume. If some element of the cost is fixed in relation to the driver or increases less than proportionately with it then the cost rate will fall. However, the organizations' total costs will have risen, often completely unnecessarily, if employees simply engineer the cost driver increases to make apparent improvements in their performance.

The impact of ABC data on performance therefore requires some monitoring by management to assess its real effects. Indeed these may only become apparent in the longer-term. For example, the Tektronix case outlined above may have shown success in short-term cost reduction but will the new system stifle designer initiative and perhaps lead to a reduction in innovation and the technological advance of the company's products?

CUSTOMER PROFITABILITY

It is normal accounting practice to recognize the realization of profit only when the sale of goods or services has been effected. Thus it is the sales transaction with the customer which is at the centre of reported profitability. However, accounting convention has rarely focused on the relationship with particular customers as the basis for identifying and reporting on profit. Rather, profitability has been reported in aggregate terms for the entity or segmented on the basis of operational divisions or product lines. However, the customer provides a perspective for analysing profit which focuses directly on the market and provides a valuable input into decision making at a strategic level.

In order to produce analyses of customer profitability both revenue and costs must be associated with customers. The former is easily achieved through the normal sales and debtors accounting systems. The latter requires that the customer becomes the cost object. It is at this stage that ABC can play a part in facilitating the production of reliable customer profitability information. ABC product costs provide a starting point, but even at this level any customization of products (e.g. involving the use of special technical modifications or presenta-

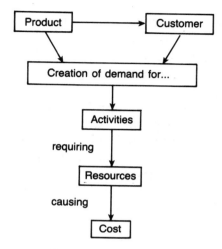

Figure 9.2 Customer influence on cost.

tional attributes) should be identified and reflected in the costs used. Traditionally, the remaining non-production costs (e.g. sales, marketing, distribution) have been attached to product cost as a standard percentage based on the costs themselves or the selling price of the product. This approach is quick and convenient but will frequently fail to reflect how the product has consumed the underlying resources in these areas when being sold to particular customers. The ABC methodology rectifies this deficiency by recognizing that the customer as well as the product is the ultimate driver for significant business costs (Figure 9.2).

Customer-driven non-production costs can be highly significant in many industries (Bellis-Jones, 1989). As with many production overheads, they can be viewed as activity-based pools of cost, including sales force work, distribution (both channel and method), warehousing, warranties and post-sale attention and financing. The customer characteristics which can influence the demand for these activities will include the type of distribution channel used to service the customer (e.g. mail order, retail, etc.), the size of the customer (e.g. larger customers may be offered special discounts), the location of the customer (e.g. exporting may require considerably more administrative effort than home sales). Thus, funding cost drivers for these activities and using the ABC methodology to attach their costs to products can produce some novel information for management.

Reported instances of the application of these ideas have shown novel and unexpected patterns of profitability at the level of customer orientation. For example, particular distribution channels geared to customer types have exhibited their relative probabilities for the first time [Winchell Lighting Case in Cooper and Kaplan (1991)], certain classes of customer which appear highly profitable at a level of profitability utilizing only production costs have become loss makers when non-production costs were included in the computation (Bellis-Jones, 1989) and the distribution of profits among customers has indicated that a relatively small proportion of customers often accounts for a majority of the overall profit, as illustrated in Figure 9.3 [Kanthal Case in Cooper and Kaplan, (1991)].

This analysis identifies those customers who are making the greatest contribution to the profitability and conversely those (the final 80% in Figure 9.3) who are loss makers. This perspective management can contribute to the managerial strategy on customer relationships, for example the identification of those

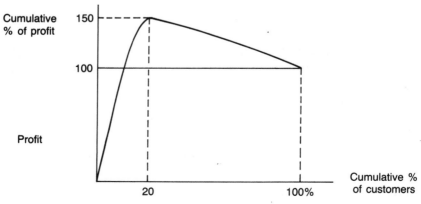

Fig. 9.3

with whom links must be maintained and fostered, or pin-pointing the need to modify the relationship with others per-haps through amending discounts or delivery arrangements or possibly the termination of business with certain customers.

CONCLUSION

The above applications of ABC demonstrate its significant and wide-ranging potential as a basis for effective cost manage-ment. The ABC approach generates a variety of information which allows management to view their organization's cost structure from a novel and highly relevant perspective. The primary orientation, in simple terms, is to reveal, 'what they are getting for the money that is spent'. It therefore allows them to view costs clearly in relation to what is happening operationally in the firm and so emphasizes the causality of cost in a way which can guide management action. Therefore, ABC has great value in managerial attention directing and decision making at various levels.

ABC can provide information relevant to the control and monitoring of operations at the operational level (e.g. non-financial cost driver monitoring), it can provide guidance at the tactical level of managerial policy (e.g. guidance on cost reduction through the elimination or reduction of non-value-added activities as a move toward the achievement of low cost production targets) and it can also benefit management in the establishment of strategic policy (e.g. the financial assessment of the product range and the customer profile).

While these potential benefits provide a strong case for, at the least, a serious consideration of ABC, like any accounting ap-proach or technique it is not, of itself, a panacea which will solve all managerial problems. Generating the basic data is a sensitive issue among employees, particularly so where staff reductions are perceived as likely. The information itself does not overcome all of the technical allocation problems of cost accounting and being a cost-based approach it does not direct-ly provide information on the future cash flow implications of decisions. It should therefore be used with these caveat's in mind and as an aid to directing managerial attention to areas of attention which can then be explored and investigated more fully.

REFERENCES

Bellis-Jones, R. (1989) Customer profitability analysis. *Management Accounting (UK)*, February, **67**, 26–8.

Bellis-Jones, R. and Hand, M. (1989) Seeking out the profit dissipations. *Management Accounting (UK)*, September, **67**, 48–50.

Cooper, R. and Kaplan, R. S. (1991) *The Design of Cost Management Systems*, Prentice-Hall, Englewood Cliffs, New Jersey.

Develin *et al.*, *Activity Based Cost Management*, Develin and Partners, London.

Hiromoto, T. (1988) Another hidden edge: Japanese management accounting. *Harvard Business Review*, July/August, **66**, 22–6.

Horngren, C. T. (1967) A contribution margin approach to the analysis of capacity utilisation. *The Accounting Review*, April, Vol. 42, 254–64.

Innes, J. and Mitchell, F. (1990) *Activity Based Costing: a review with case studies*, CIMA, London.

Johnson, H. T. (1988) Activity based information: a blueprint for world class management accounting. *Management Accounting (USA)*, June, **69**, 23–30.

Jonez, J. W. and Wright, M. A. (1987) Material burdening: management accounting can support competitive strategy. *Management Accounting (USA)*, August, **69**, 27–31.

Morley, M. (1978) *The Value Added Statement*, ICAS, Edinburgh.

Solomons, D. (1968) The analysis of standard cost variances, in *Studies in Cost Analysis* (ed. D. Solomons), Sweet and Maxwell, London, pp. 426–43.

CHAPTER TEN

Stocks and throughput

INTRODUCTION

The nature of cost is such that the adage 'time is money' is one which can be highly appropriate to cost management. Once funds have been committed to the acquisition of a resource then, other things being equal, the faster it can be utilized to generate sales revenue from finished output, the greater the financial benefits derived from the whole operation. These benefits stem from the increased volume of saleable output which an increased production and sales velocity permit and from the earlier command which it gives the seller over cash. Thus, improving the rate of resource conversion and sale should be a key component of any cost management strategy. It is a factor which can be primarily influenced in two ways:

(1) resources should be acquired as near as possible to the time of their use;
(2) the conversion and selling processes should be undertaken as quickly as possible.

Policies designed to achieve these aims have recently received considerable publicity. The just-in-time (JIT) approach to purchasing and production provides a philosophy and practice of demand-driven acquisition and use of resource. Throughput accounting emphasizes the management of given resources to improve the rate at which raw materials are transformed into sales. Both can therefore contribute to this type of cost management effort.

THE JIT CONCEPT

The existence of inventory confers several benefits on an organization. It provides a buffer which in the case of finished goods and work in progress facilitates the delivery of output to customers on time and in the case of raw materials contributes to the avoidance of production stoppages. In inflationary conditions it also allows the organization to benefit from holding gains through buying early. However, the former benefits only represent real benefits where it is not possible to organize procurement, production and selling activities to be quickly responsive to customer demand. Where a customer order can trigger the initial acquisition of necessary resources and they can be converted fast enough to deliver on time to the customer then the carrying of stocks and work in progress becomes a non-value-added characteristic of the business. The ability to operate with the minimum of stocks will therefore be dependent on having a secure and efficient source of timeous material supplies which are of a satisfactory quality and on organizing production resources to ensure that hold-ups and stoppages become negligible and processing lead time is short.

If organizing in this way is possible then a JIT philosophy is financially attractive as the benefits of holding stock are largely lost and the following costs and risks, all of which are associated with stockholding, are avoided:

(1) the risk of damaging stocks;
(2) the risk of stocks becoming obsolete;
(3) the opportunity cost of tying funds up in stocks;
(4) the costs of storing and moving stocks internally;
(5) the risk of holding losses (where supply prices are falling).

The basic JIT approach is outlined in Figure 10.1, which shows the customer initiating and driving the activity within the supplying organization in a way which will promptly meet de-

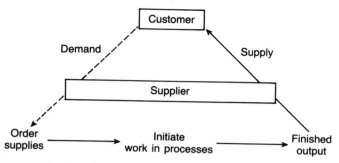

Figure 10.1 The just-in-time concept.

mand. Purchasing has to be arranged so that suitable materials are available just as the first work cell or department in the production process is ready for them. For this to be achieved good communications must be established with suppliers (perhaps through computer link-ups) and supplier reliability in providing what is ordered at the appropriate time is essential. Daily or even hourly deliveries may be required. In Japan, subcontractors locate in close proximity to manufacturers in order to provide just such a flexible service. The need for quality from suppliers is also intensified for faulty supplies hold up the whole process. Developing quality assurance mechanisms in partnership with suppliers is not unusual among large producers involved in JIT programmes. In order to assess the continuity of supply the purchasing company's accountants may also become involved in assessing the supplier's financial viability. Although the purchase costs of supplies from sources which can satisfy these requirements may exceed those available elsewhere the benefits of JIT will often outweigh them so creating a demand for secure, quick and flexible supplies.

In the production process activity should be guided on a demand–pull basis. The creation of work in a department or work cell comes only from a demand for its output from those which succeed it and ultimately this demand derives from external sales orders. To work efficiently an appropriate layout which streamlines the movement of work in process is necessary. Productive resources (labour and capital equipment) must be scheduled for availability when needed and efforts made to eliminate bottlenecks and reduce production lead time.

JIT AND ACCOUNTING

Conventional cost control systems do not fit well with the JIT concept (Maskell, 1986; McNair *et al.*, 1988; Harris, 1990). Standard cost efficiency, usage and volume variances are all geared to making use of resources which are available for production. This motivates production staff to produce stock where no final demand currently exists so that unfavourable cost variances are not created. It thus clashes with the basic no stock philosophy of JIT. Furthermore, efficiency variances are frequently segmented by production department or work cell. However, where JIT ideas are operational these are all linked together by the pull of final demand. Thus if a problem, say a machine breakdown, occurs at an early stage in the process all subsequent work centres are also held up. These too will therefore produce unfavourable efficiency and volume variances but cannot be viewed as responsible for them. The use of these measures to assess performance which is outside managerial control is not only misleading but can be demoralizing to staff. Consequently, accounting systems and measures require modification to accommodate the JIT approach. No standard accounting system exists for this but some suggestions for the types of contribution which can be made by accounting are outlined below.

Focus on stocks and work in progress

The reporting of stock levels becomes important as stock reduction and elimination lies at the heart of JIT. Thus it is important for management to monitor closely in this area. Conventionally, stocks will simply be split into raw material, work-in-progress and finished goods and reported in this way. In order to facilitate management's assessment of progress towards JIT it will be useful to also report on the following dimensions of stockholding.

(1) The stockholding analysed by product type to identify where in the product range JIT is proving difficult to implement.
(2) The stockholding analysed by physical location to show where in the production process buffers appear to be needed.
(3) The stockholding may be aged by date of acquisition to help judge how near to usage time stocks have been acquired and to identify and investigate any anomalies.
(4) To further analyse the lead time between acquisition and use, the stockholding can be projected forward to show when it is expected to be used and any exceptional lead time can be investigated.

In order to help emphasize that stockholding costs money it might also be possible to impute a charge to all stock representing the real cost of funds which are invested in it. If the organization's cost of capital were 10% per annum, and at 31 December a category of finished goods was costed as shown in column 1 of Table 10.1, then the imputed charge would be £450. This would be a charge which would increase with the amount of stock and the lead time between its acquisition and final sale. By increasing the denominator of the return on investment ratio before sale and the cost of sales figure after sale it would penalize the holding and growth of inventory. Finally,

Table 10.1 Stock: an inputted time cost

	Product x (£)	Imputed charge (funds invested × cost of capital × proportion of year)	Revised cost (£)
Direct material (purchased 30 June)	5000	+ (£5000 × 0.1 × 0.5)	5250
Direct labour (incurred evenly Sept.–Oct.)	4000	+ (£4000 × 0.1 × 0.25)	4100
Overhead (incurred evenly Sept.–Dec.)	6000	+ (£6000 × 0.1 × 0.17)	6100
	15 000		15 450

it may be possible to utilize the ideas of activity-based costing (ABC) to identify all the costs of poor supplier performance. This would be done by adding to the purchase cost of each supplier the cost of activities caused by material handling and storage, late delivery and substandard supplies.

Critical success factors

If JIT is to be successful the organization of production has to be sound. In order to monitor and motivate improvements in this area a set of factors critical to the system's ability to respond in a JIT manner should be reported. These would include:

(1) the production lead time for products and its segmentation for each stage throughout the production process including non-processing time;
(2) the ratio of work time to total time in the process for each type of product;
(3) set-up time;
(4) the analysis of rejects, rework, scrap;
(5) the time spent on quality assessment and prevention together with the costs of internal and external failure;
(6) schedule adherence performance.

Bottlenecks

Constraints on the flow of production leading to the satisfaction of final demand should be identified by observation, analysing capacity usage (bottlenecks should always be in use 100% of the time) and pin-pointing hold-ups in the system. This allows the use of the bottleneck to be scheduled in the way which will best benefit profitability and also directs managerial attention at the obvious need for capital investment to alleviate the constraint.

Costing simplification

One spin-off benefit of JIT systems has been the reduction of the importance of investment in work-in-progress. Coupled with the reduction in the significance of direct labour (in many electronics firms it is well below 5% of production cost) a simplification in product costing procedures has become possible. This is achieved by attaching costs only to finished output and abandoning any attempt to track and cost work-in-process through the production system. Thus only when finished production is notified are costs transferred from the individual cost element (materials, overheads) accounts to cost it. Direct labour (due to its insignificance) and overheads are usually merged in one rate which simplifies the process further. 'Backflushing' is the term used for this type of costing [see Foster and Horngren (1987) and Cocker (1989) for a more detailed description].

THE NATURE OF THROUGHPUT ACCOUNTING

Throughput accounting (TA) is an approach to accounting which is largely in sympathy with the JIT philosophy. In essence, TA assumes that a manager has a given set of resources available. These comprise existing buildings, capital equipment and labour force. Using these resources, purchased materials and parts must be processed to generate sales revenue. Given this scenario the most appropriate financial objective to set for doing this is the maximization of throughput (Goldratt and Cox, 1984) which is defined as:

sales revenue **less** direct material cost.

As the cost of all other factors are deemed fixed, this objective will motivate management to generate the greatest profit for the business. It is an approach which has already generated substantial benefits for several businesses (Schmenner, 1988; Darlington *et al.*, 1992).

Throughput as defined above can be influenced in four ways:

(1) selling price;
(2) direct material purchase price;
(3) usage of direct material;
(4) volume of throughput.

Thus managerial attention is focused on these four key areas. They have strong interrelationships (e.g. between selling price and throughput volume and between direct material quality and selling price) which have to be balanced in determining the practical policies which will benefit total throughput. Clearly it is also an approach which links with JIT as, by definition, throughput is not directly generated by producing for stock but only by effecting sales from finished output. However, to the extent that the existence of stocks enhance the possibility of creating and increasing throughput then, within the TA approach, they can be viewed as desirable. Stocks must therefore be monitored carefully and in a way which facilitates this type of assessment of them.

In order to promote throughput it is necessary to start by identifying the factors which are currently limiting its expansion. These are normally termed constraints. They relate to the circumstances of the organization and might include the following types of factor:

(1) the existence of an uncompetitive selling price;
(2) the need to deliver on time to particular customers;
(3) the lack of product quality and reliability;
(4) the lack of reliable material supplies;
(5) the existence of shortages of production resources.

Management strategy and policies can then be directed at the alleviation of the constraints. Within the production facility itself constraints caused by a lack of production resources (e.g. shortages of machining capacity) are termed bottlenecks. To increase throughput they have to be identified and eliminated. This can be done by the transfer of existing resources within the factory or by investment in new resources. Indeed the applicability of the throughput concept in setting the capital investment programme is deemed one of its big advantages and one which is commonly overlooked where TA is not used. However, the elimination of one internal bottleneck will normally result in the creation of another at a previously satisfactory location. Thus the management of bottlenecks becomes a primary concern of the manager seeking to increase throughput. The accountant's role in this type of system still lacks explicit definition but should involve addressing the following factors.

Throughput end-result measurement

Periodic profit measurements can be supplemented by a statement of throughput which may also show how the throughput has been consumed (Table 10.2). In this way the success of management in increasing throughput can be monitored through examination of its trend over time. Moreover the generation of throughput can be segmented to show how individual products are contributing to it and so guide the management's product mix policies. Indeed, where variable costs other than direct materials are small this type of measurement will closely approximate contribution analysis, the normal basis for short-term volume-oriented decisions.

Table 10.2 Throughput report[a]

		£
Sales		x
Direct materials		(x)
Throughput		x
Direct labour	(x)	
Production overhead	(x)	
Administration costs	(x)	
Selling expenses	(x)	(x)
Operation profit		x

[a] This implies the costing of any stocks or work in progress at direct material cost.

Identifying bottlenecks

The profiling of capacity usage throughout a production facility can help in identifying bottlenecks, as they will normally be the areas most heavily used. In addition, the build-up of work in progress in advance of an operation suggests a restriction to the free flow of production. Thus monitoring stock by location can be useful. Alternatively, idle-time and waiting time at operations may indicate bottlenecks in forthcoming operations.

Reporting on bottlenecks

At bottlenecks the efficiency of operations assumes an added significance. Processing ability becomes directly relevant to throughput generation and any variation in efficiency at these points has a direct effect on throughput. Thus the measurement of efficiency and a quick awareness of changes in it provides valuable information for bottleneck management. Furthermore the need to ensure the full employment of bottleneck resources may lead to the need for a pre-bottleneck stock of work in process to be maintained and monitored. Finally, the prioritizing of work at bottlenecks may be based on its ability to generate throughput. Thus throughput per bottleneck capacity measures, such as machine hours or labour hours, for different product lines would constitute the basis for a ranking of this sort to be done.

Lead times

Providing the demand exists any increases in the rate at which production volume can be generated by the conversion process will improve throughput. Thus the reduction of lead times, set-up times and waiting times can all benefit throughput. The ability to adhere to pre-set production schedules designed to maximize throughput will also be important. Reporting these factors will help to focus on them and to promote and assess their improvement.

Other factors

The accounting measurement system should also support the need to take action with respect to all constraints. Thus if quality constrains performance then quality cost reports, rework, scrap and returns should all be central to the performance, measurement and reporting function. If delivery on time is crucial then data on performance in this area has to be gathered. The system of reporting in a TA system should be designed to suit the requirements of the situation and will therefore be contingent on the nature of the constraints and circumstances of the organization involved.

THROUGHPUT ACCOUNTING ASSESSMENT

A system of TA should support the objective of maximizing throughput. It should sharpen managements' focus on the factors critical to the attainment of this aim. It is therefore an approach which will, in many respects, mirror the JIT idea where speed and flexibility of production are paramount. It will be particularly pertinent in firms where direct material is a highly significant cost element (as other resources and costs are treated as given or fixed) and where final demand is high enough and constant enough to place continuous pressure on available production resources. It is an approach which simplifies the situation confronting management, and while this can be beneficial in clarifying, highlighting and prioritizing a few key issues it may also lead to complications where the assumptions underlying simplification do not hold good.

In this respect, TA adopts a highly short-term perspective in its classification and assumption on costs, all of which, except material, are deemed given or fixed. Furthermore, as the computation of throughput excludes costs other than direct material the motivation for management to focus on and attend to these other elements of cost is diminished. Thus whole areas of cost incurrence may be relatively neglected. Indeed the assumption that all labour and overheads will always be fixed even in the short term is also questionable and where variable costs other than material exist then throughput maximization will lead to suboptimization of profit (Figure 10.2).

The strengths of TA therefore lie in its concentration upon the responsiveness of the production facility to meet final demand for its output. Its weaknesses lie in its lack of concern for costs

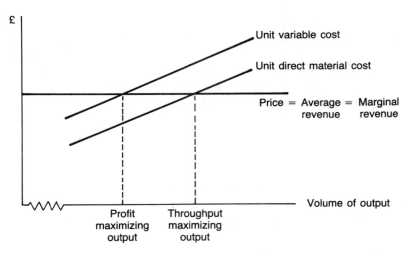

Figure 10.2 Throughput maximization versus profit maximization.

other than direct material. However, these characteristics make it a good complement for ABC where the focus is on labour and overhead costs. In combination the approaches therefore provide a reasonably comprehensive coverage of the spread of costs.

CONCLUSION

The ideas of reducing stocks and increasing production velocity can themselves be of substantial financial benefit to those organizations which can effectively put them into practice. In addition, the operation of the business in this way forces management to address and solve many other problems which a move to the JIT/TA philosophies will highlight. First, production management has to be developed to cope with bottlenecks, absenteeism, scheduling and the effective balancing of resources. Second, there is a need for total quality management to be embraced to ensure the smooth flow of good output. Third, the availability of operating capacity has to be ensured by policies of total preventative maintenance. All of these 'spin-off' benefits contribute to the potential for improvement inherent in lowering stocks and raising throughput.

REFERENCES

Cocker, M. (1989) Financial management and just-in-time. *Management Accounting (UK)*, September, **67**, 46–7.

Darlington, J., Innes, J., Mitchell, F. and Woodward, J. (1992) Throughput accounting: the Garrett automotive experience. *Management Accounting (UK)*, **70**, 32–5 and 38.

Foster, G. and Horngren, C.T., (1987) JIT: cost accounting and cost management issues. *Management Accounting (USA)*, June, **68**, 19–25.

Goldratt, E. and Cox, J. (1984) *The Goal*, Gower. Alderzhot.

Harris, E. (1990) The impact of JIT production on product cost information systems. *Production and Inventory Management Journal*, First Quarter, 44–8.

Maskell, B. (1986) Management accounting and just-in-time. *Management Accounting (UK)*, September, **64**, 32–4.

McNair, C.J., Mosconi, W. and Norris, T. (1988) *Meeting the Technology Challenge: cost accounting in a JIT environment*, National Association of Accountants/Coopers & Lybrand.

Schmenner, R.W. (1988) The merit of making things fast. *Sloan Management Review*, Fall. **30**, 11–17.

CHAPTER ELEVEN

Strategic management accounting

INTRODUCTION

This book reviews a number of modern cost management approaches including target costing, functional analysis, cost estimation, cost tables and activity-based costing. While these techniques can be considered important in their own right they also provide the basis of an accounting input to organizational strategy. The significance of what might be termed strategic management accounting has been increasingly recognized in recent years as the discipline has developed the approaches which can generate suitable information on the cost management aspects of strategy.

It follows that just as different organizations have different strategies, so different organizations should have different cost management systems to support their particular strategies. For example, if the strategy is to become one of the lowest cost producers of a particular product, the cost management system might be designed to help achieve the reduction of production and other costs. In contrast, if the strategy is to aim for product differentiation, the cost management system could aid such a strategy by supporting design innovation and variation, perhaps by ensuring experimentation, research and development are all encouraged and rewarded rather than penalized by the costing system.

However, the strategic decision process is complex. Mintzberg *et al.* (1976) argued that 'strategic decision processes are immensely complex and dynamic and yet . . . they are amenable to conceptual structuring'. Management accounting has therefore to be innovative and responsive if it is to fit this type of function. One distinguishing feature of strategic management accounting is the primarily external focus on gathering information about the organization's environment. This contrasts with the mainly internal focus of many traditional management accounting techniques. Relevant external information would include shifts in customer demand, technological changes, physical environmental considerations, new governmental regulations, industry benchmarking, and competitors' actions. Traditional management accounting does not produce this type of information, although it appears to comprise the basis of financial reports to top level management. For example, the KPMG (1990) survey of information for strategic management found that 'information currently provided to executive boards is biased towards financial indicators and concentrates on internal self-determined comparisons'.

To develop a strategic dimension management accountants need to provide a range of financial and non-financial performance measures and external comparisons as part of the information on which strategic decisions can be made. Figure 11.1 attempts to place strategic management accounting in context by considering different levels of planning and control (i.e. strategic planning, management control and operational control) in relation to the product life cycle. For example, at the operational control level during the production stage in the product life cycle, standard costing would be one technique which would fall into box C. Budgeting is a technique which would fall into box B at the management control level during the preparation for the production stage. However, whereas several techniques in traditional management accounting fall into boxes B and C, box A (strategic planning at the embryo stage of the product life cycle) is relatively bare with few traditional management accounting techniques. Many of the techniques outlined in earlier chapters can be used to rectify this deficiency. This chapter considers briefly additional relatively recent developments which can help fill this gap. Shareholder

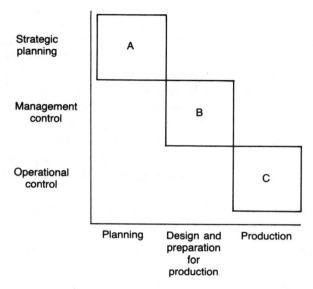

Figure 11.1 Management control and product life cycle.

value analysis, value chain analysis, non-financial performance measures and product life cycle costing all relate to cost
management issues and can contribute to box A type management accounting inputs.

SHAREHOLDER VALUE ANALYSIS

In the corporate sector a critical test for evaluating company
strategy is whether a proposed strategy creates value for shareholders. The basic problem is finding an operational definition
for 'value for shareholders'. Rappaport (1981, p. 39) has written extensively in this area of shareholder value analysis with
the objective of providing 'top management and board members with a theoretically sound, practical approach for assessing the contribution of strategic business unit (SBU) plans and
overall corporate strategic plans towards creating economic
value for shareholders'. Rappaport (1986) suggests the use of
'value drivers'. Mills (1990) describes how the Quaker Oats

Company (Annual Reports, 1988 and 1989) have used this concept. This organization emphasizes three value drivers which are critical for value to shareholders through their impact on the company's ability to generate cash. The three value drivers identified are sales growth, operating profit margin and investment with the cash position being determined by their relationship of sales × profit margin − investment. The impact of alternative strategies on these three value drivers is crucial to top level decision making. However, another important value driver is the cost of capital which is used to assess the value of future cash generation.

The effects of these value drivers can be seen by considering two aspects of shareholder value:

(1) the present value of net cash flows from the operations of the business during a given planning period; and
(2) the 'residual value' of the operations of the business which is its present value for the period beyond the current planning period under review.

To calculate the final shareholder value of the strategies for the planning period, the market value of debt and any other claims would be deducted from the total of (1) and (2) above and the value of any other non-operational sources of value would be added. The second component of shareholder value, namely the 'residual value', is a critical element of shareholder value analysis as it is a useful counterbalance to discourage short-term strategies such as reducing advertising, training or research and development costs. However, the problem with residual value is that it can be calculated in a number of different ways. For example, Rappaport proposes a perpetuity assumption but residual values can also be calculated based on the price earnings ratio or on a comparison of the stock market and value of the firm.

Rappaport's method based on the idea of discounted cash flows has similarities with the approach to strategic financial management proposed by Allen (1988a). Again Allen emphasizes the financial management of the business over the long-term. Allen (1988b) suggests the cost of capital should be adopted as the discount rate and strategic financial management 'looks at present values at three levels:

(1) individual dimensions of strategy (e.g. pricing, advertising, quality, mechanization);
(2) the balance of dimensions across an identifiable business unit (e.g. how does a high quality, high price advertised strategy compare with a low quality, low price unadvertised one);
(3) the blending of business into an effective corporate enterprise (taking advantage of synergies, e.g. economies of scale)'.

This approach based on the future cash flow implications of strategy provides a sound basis for ensuring that strategic decisions are based on relevant financial information and will conform to the objective of economically benefiting the owner or shareholder.

VALUE CHAIN ANALYSIS

In the management literature Porter (1985) identified the 'value chain' which is the linked set of value-creating activities from raw material sourcing to the final product or service being delivered to the customer. Shank and Govindarajan (1992) have shown how strategic cost management, with a focus external to the organization, can help in the management of an organization's value chain. They suggest that 'the value chain framework is a method for breaking down the chain – from basic raw materials to end-use customers – into strategically relevant activities to understand the behaviour of costs and the sources of differentiation'. A three-step approach for the value chain methodology is used by them. The first step is to construct the industry's value chain, to identify the various activities within the value chain and to relate operating costs, revenues and assets to individual value activities. The second step is to determine the cost drivers which affect costs in each value activity. Basically these are related to the cost drivers discussed previously under the heading of activity-based costing and management but viewed in a wider strategic context. For example, volume is only one of many cost drivers. Shank and Govindarajan (1992) classify these into two categories: structural cost drivers and executional cost drivers. Structural cost drivers relate to the strategic decisions which an organization makes about its fundamental economic characteristics. The following areas comprise structural cost drivers:

(1) scale;
(2) scope (degree of vertical integration);
(3) experience;
(4) technology;
(5) complexity (number of different types of products or services sold).

Executional cost drivers relate to an organization's ability to deliver the product or service successfully to the customer. Shank and Govindarajan argue that more is always better for the following executional cost drivers:

(1) employee participation;
(2) total quality management;
(3) capacity utilization;
(4) plant layout efficiency;
(5) product configuration;
(6) links with suppliers and customers.

The third step in the value chain methodology is to develop sustainable competitive advantage. This can be achieved by reducing costs whilst maintaining value (sales) or increasing value (sales) whilst maintaining costs or some combination of the two. At this stage the cost management system provides a critical input to the strategic decision-making process. It should provide guidance on how to improve a firm's value chain to gain sustainable competitive advantage. To achieve this requires a deep understanding of not only ones own firm's value chain but also the value chains of competitors.

The value chain is another example of a technique with an external emphasis not only in relation to competitors but also back to suppliers and forward to customers. The interdependence of the value chain must be understood before effective strategic decisions can be taken, guided and supported to a large extent by the organization's cost management system.

NON-FINANCIAL PERFORMANCE MEASURES

At first sight it may seem strange to include a section on non-financial performance indicators in a book on cost management. However, non-financial measures can give indications of resource consumption patterns and hence cost incurrence. Thus the easiest way to manage costs is often to measure, report and control the physical variables which can mean more than money amounts in practical managerial terms. Non-financial performance measures can cover various areas such as quality, delivery, market standing and human resources. Taylor and Graham (1992) suggest the framework to combine both financial and non-financial information together with both internal and external information, shown in Table 11.1.

Table 11.1 Non-financial internal and external performance measures

		Internal		*External*	
		Past	*Future*	*Past*	*Future*
Financial	Numeric	Management accounting	Budgets and forecasts	Competitor's results	Brokers' forecasts
	Text	Results narrative	Five-year plan framework	Broker's review	Press opinion
Non-financial	Numeric	Operating performance	Capacity planning	Market share	Market research
	Text	Performance commentary	Strategic goals	Trade media coverage	Technology forecasts

The appropriate internal and external non-financial information will depend on the industry and within each industry will depend on the particular strategy of each company. Each company should know its critical success factors and measure its own performance in these areas both over time and more importantly against its competitors. Simmonds (1981, p. 26) has in fact defined strategic management accounting as 'the provision and analysis of management accounting data about a business and its competitors for use in developing and monitoring the business strategy'. Just as it is vital to consider competitors' reactions to a price change and to estimate competitors' costs and financial strength, so it is also important to monitor competitors' non-financial performance in areas such as market standing, quality and delivery. In many ways this distinction between non-financial performance measures and cost management is artificial because these two areas interact with each other. For example, many organizations conduct regular competitive analysis exercises using a team with different skills such as purchasing, production, engineering, marketing and accounting. With reverse engineering a competitor's product is analysed in detail in terms of its design, technical specifications, material content, production process, marketing features and costs. What is important is the provision of a benchmark picture of the competitor's product and both non-financial measures and costs are valuable parts of it.

PRODUCT LIFE CYCLE COSTING AND MANAGEMENT

Product life cycle costing is based on the identification and analyses of each individual product's costs throughout its entire life cycle. Thus the costs incurred at the planning, design, preparation for production, production, support and disposal stages of the product are provided. In addition, cost commitment may be analysed. Perhaps the most important point is that experience has shown that up to 90% of the producer's costs for a product are committed during the planning and design stages. That is a major reason why this book has concentrated on the development of cost management techniques which can be used during the early stages of the product life cycle.

Product life cycle costing can include different costs. For example, one approach is to examine all the costs which the producer will incur, but another wider approach is also to include all the costs which the customer will incur such as installation, operation, maintenance and disposal. An even wider approach is to include the costs caused by the product but paid in effect by society, such as pollution costs. The view of costs given by this approach is highly pertinent to sales and marketing policies. The pattern of cost incurrence at different stages in the life cycle can also assist production management where costs at one stage in the product life cycle can have a major effect on costs during subsequent stages. This applies particularly to decisions made during the planning and design stages. For example, designers can be encouraged to use the same parts in different products, to design products for easy assembly and also to minimize customers' operating, servicing and disposal costs.

Shields and Young (1991) suggest that product life cycle costs can be 'estimated by one or a combination of three methods, namely analogy, parametric models or cost accounting models'. The analogy method is based on the costs of a similar product suitably adjusted for significant differences proposed for the new product. Parametric models use a non-linear regression model with the cost as the dependent variable and independent variables such as design, manufacturing complexity and performance. The cost accounting models use the traditional cost accounting approach based on materials, labour and overheads.

As with the other costing techniques discussed in this book, product life cycle costing has important implications for cost management. Shields and Young (1991) point out that the sequential approach to design and manufacturing 'has been criticized because:

it increases the length of a product's life cycle;
it increases whole life costs;
it increases lead and delivery times; and
it decreases the product's quality'.

In many Japanese companies multidisciplinary teams work at the same time on different stages of the product life cycle rather than on each stage sequentially. Japanese companies use target costing and cost tables to help in their product life cycle management.

In a survey of nine Western firms, Shields and Young (1991) found product life cycle costing to be not particularly well developed. The systems tended to be fragmented, the training was inadequate and there was evidence of several sources of resistance to the idea of product life cycle costing: 'The existing cost accounting systems tend to be oriented too much toward reporting departmental or functional area costs rather than product whole life costs by activity. Product manufacturing costs are also emphasized at the expense of premanufacturing and postmanufacturing product activities'.

The life cycle concept supports the strategic view needed in a competitive world. It directs management attention in ways which conventional cost systems neglect and emphasizes the significance of timing decisions to meet the particular needs of individual components of the product portfolio. To be effective, however, it does require that management accountants become adaptable and are prepared to accept that traditional approaches are not sacrosanct.

TARGET COST MANAGEMENT, FUNCTIONAL ANALYSIS, COST TABLES AND ABC

This chapter has outlined some of the current management accounting approaches which can contribute to the information on which strategic decisions are taken. However, many of the techniques already discussed in the previous chapters also have strategic aspects. For example, target cost management is a cost management which looks towards the competition by starting from a market price and working back to a product cost which has to be achieved. As market price depends on the strategy of the organization, for example is it aimed at being a mass market product or a niche market product, the target cost management policy becomes a strategic management accounting technique.

Functional analysis and cost tables are two other cost management techniques with strategic elements. For example, in functional analysis a critical step is to determine the value of each function to the customer. In this way the existing internal costs can be compared against the benchmark of the customers' views to determine the aspects of the product requiring priority attention. Similarly, cost tables also include external information, for example about the costs of different materials and different production processes which are available in the resource market. Activity-based costing also has strategic implications. These exist in allowing product line costings to influence the product range offered to the market and in questioning which activities are non-value-added from the perspective of the customer. Finally, JIT and throughput provide an accounting response to modern developments in production. They can supplement a TQM approach and contribute towards the provision of a quality service to the market.

Cost management systems thus have the potential to provide a stream of valuable information to management. Cost information has clear links to many operational decisions but as shown above it can also be designed to contribute to longer-term decision making which sets the organization's marketplace strategy.

REFERENCES

Allen, D. (1988a) *Strategic Financial Management: managing for long-term financial success*, Financial Times Business Information.

Allen, D. (1988b) The hitchhikers guide to strategic financial management. *Management Accounting*, October, **66**, 12–13.

KPMG Management Consultants (1990) *A Survey of Leading Companies 1990 – Information for Strategic Management*.

Mills, R.W. (1990) Strategic financial management and shareholder value analysis. *Management Accounting (UK)*, March, **68**, 36–8.

Mintzberg, H., Raisinghani, D. and Theoret, A. (1976) The structure of "unstructured" decision processes. *Administrative Science Quarterly*, June, **21**, 246–75.

Porter, M.E. (1985) *Competitive Advantage: creating and sustaining superior performance*, The Free Press, New York.

Rappaport, A. (1981) Selecting strategies that create shareholder value. *Harvard Business Review*, May/June, **59**, 139–49.

Rappaport, A. (1986) *Creating Shareholder Value: the new standard for business performance*, The Free Press, New York.

Shank, J.K. and Govindarajan, V. (1992) Strategic cost management and the value chain, in *Handbook of Cost Management* (ed. B.J. Brinker), Warren Gorham & Lamont, Boston, pp. D1-1 to D1-37.

Shields, M.D. and Young, S.M. (1991) Managing product life cycle costs: an organizational model. *Journal of Cost Management*, Fall, **5**(3), 39–52.

Simmonds, K. (1981) Strategic management accounting. *Management Accounting (UK)*, **59**(4), April, 26–9.

Taylor, B. and Graham, C. (1992) Information for strategic management. *Management Accounting (UK)*, January, **70**, 52–4.

CHAPTER TWELVE

Conclusions

MANAGEMENT ACCOUNTING CHANGE

It has been argued that traditional management accounting lacks relevance to management in the contemporary business context (Johnson and Kaplan, 1987). If relevance is to be regained then management accounting has to change at the level of the firm. In order for this to be achieved management accountants have to:

(1) appreciate the salient characteristics and circumstances of their organization;
(2) maintain a contact with management which will allow them to acquire a knowledge of their changing information requirements;
(3) possess an awareness of the existing possibilities for information generation which the discipline offers and/or be innovative enough to develop new approaches and adapt existing ones to suit current management needs.

While all three are prerequisites for achieving an ongoing internal relevance for management accounting a book of this nature can primarily only contribute directly to the third factor. The first two involve the organization of the accounting function (decentralization), the job experience given to accountants (the possibility of job rotation) and the degree of integration achieved in linking accountants into the management processes (the use of multidisciplinary project teams). However, if management accounting practice is to actually develop within any organization the change process must be managed like any other. In exploring the process of management accounting change, Innes and Mitchell (1990) found that three sets of influences were involved.

(1) Motivators: background factors positively encouraging change over the medium- to long-term, not usually sufficient in themselves to result in change occurring, e.g. developing production technology, competition.

(2) Facilitators: internal conditions which represent potential hurdles to change, e.g. staff and computing resources available to the management accounting function.

(3) Catalysts: factors triggering an actual change, e.g. a loss being made, a new market entrant or the arrival of a new accountant.

Thus to promote change and enhance relevance, management accountants should be exposed to the motivators and catalysts but must also be provided with the facilitating conditions which permit change to occur. Hopefully a text such as this will contribute to change by acting as a catalyst within the organizations of its readers.

KEY AREAS OF EMPHASIS

The techniques outlined in this book provide a range of highly practical developments which can, at least, provide a valuable supplement to the types of traditional practices outlined in Chapter 3. They represent many of the contemporary responses to regaining 'relevance lost'. All have been developed and used within real world organizations and are considered successful by their users. While diverse in nature and application they have two particular features in common. First, they can and are being applied at the stage of taking the decisions which

commit an organization to acquiring and using particular resources. This is the stage at which the management accountant
can be most effective in contributing to cost management. This
does not preclude their use at subsequent stages in the product
life cycle although their impact then may well be less significant.
Second, they are geared towards providing an interface between
internal accounting information and the external market in
which the organization is competing. In this manner cost management becomes relevant at a strategic level and helps guide
cost commitment and cost reduction decisions in a way which
will enhance competitiveness in the medium- to long-term.

FINAL COMMENT

During the last decade many practising management accountants will have been surrounded by change: internally in
production technology and methods, in organization structure, in product or service output and life cycle, and externally
in market scope, scale and competitiveness. Many of these
changes are factors which one would expect to be central influences on the design of management accounting systems.

From this environment the management accountant will experience a strong pressure to react, to show responsiveness and
change from the traditional approaches largely developed
within another era. This book is designed to provide managers
and management accountants with some ideas as to the forms
which that change could take. Hopefully these can assist by
providing a contribution to the revision of cost management
methods and help the management accountant make a creative
and positive contribution to the future development of his/her
organization.

REFERENCES

Innes, J. and Mitchell, F. (1990) The process of change in management
accounting: 'some field study evidence'. *Management Accounting
Research*, **1**(1), 3–19.

Johnson, T. and Kaplan, R.S. (1987) *Relevance Lost – The Rise and Fall of Management Accounting*, Harvard Business School Press, Boston.

Subject index